It Happened to Me

Series Editor: Arlene Hirschfelder

Books in the It Happened to Me series are designed for inquisitive teens digging for answers about certain illnesses, social issues, or lifestyle interests. Whether you are deep into your teen years or just entering them, these books are gold mines of up-to-date information, riveting teen views, and great visuals to help you figure out stuff. Besides special boxes highlighting singular facts, each book is enhanced with the latest reading lists, websites, and an index. Perfect for browsing, there are loads of expert information by acclaimed writers to help parents, guardians, and librarians understand teen illness, tough situations, and lifestyle choices.

1. *Epilepsy: The Ultimate Teen Guide,* by Kathlyn Gay and Sean McGarrahan, 2002.
2. *Stress Relief: The Ultimate Teen Guide*, by Mark Powell, 2002.
3. *Learning Disabilities: The Ultimate Teen Guide,* by Penny Hutchins Paquette and Cheryl Gerson Tuttle, 2003.
4. *Making Sexual Decisions: The Ultimate Teen Guide,* by L. Kris Gowen, 2003.
5. *Asthma: The Ultimate Teen Guide,* by Penny Hutchins Paquette, 2003.
6. *Cultural Diversity-Conflicts and Challenges: The Ultimate Teen Guide,* by Kathlyn Gay, 2003.
7. *Diabetes: The Ultimate Teen Guide,* by Katherine J. Moran, 2004.
8. *When Will I Stop Hurting? Teens, Loss, and Grief: The Ultimate Teen Guide to Dealing with Grief,* by Ed Myers, 2004.
9. *Volunteering: The Ultimate Teen Guide,* by Kathlyn Gay, 2004.
10. *Organ Transplants—A Survival Guide for the Entire Family: The Ultimate Teen Guide,* by Tina P. Schwartz, 2005.

Immigration

The Ultimate Teen Guide

TATYANA KLEYN

It Happened to Me, No. 29

The Scarecrow Press, Inc.
Lanham • Toronto • Plymouth, UK
2011

Published by Scarecrow Press, Inc.
A wholly owned subsidary of The Rowman & Littlefield Publishing Group, Inc.
4501 Forbes Boulevard, Suite 200, Lanham, Maryland 20706
http://www.scarecrowpress.com

Estover Road, Plymouth PL6 7PY, United Kingdom

British Library Cataloguing in Publication Information Available

Library of Congress Cataloging-in-Publication Data
Kleyn, Tatyana.
 Immigration : the ultimate teen guide / Tatyana Kleyn.
   p. cm. — (It happened to me ; No. 29)
 Includes bibliographical references and index.
 ISBN 978-0-8108-6984-4 (hardcover : alk. paper) — ISBN 978-0-8108-6999-8 (ebook)
 1. United States—Emigration and immigration. 2. Immigrants—United States. I. Title.
 JV6465.K54 2011
 304.8'73—dc22   2010038930

To my loving parents—
Fanya Mozeshtam and Jack Kleyn

In of honor of Edgard Mercado Meneses (1970–2009)—
a friend, teacher, and immigrant

Contents

Acknowledgments

This book would not have been possible without the support and encouragement of my colleagues, students, friends, and family. I have learned so much working on this project and owe a great deal to those who responded to the many inquiries. My student at The City College of New York (CCNY), Jaqueline Cinto, has been on this journey with me from the very start. Jaqueline has spent endless hours conducting research to ensure the most updated information, and she also contributed to the related resources sections. I cannot say enough about my friend and colleague Nancy Stern, who read many of the chapters and offered her precise feedback to keep the book moving along. Arlene Hirschfelder, the series editor, supported me throughout the writing process and answered my myriad questions. I have also benefited from the knowledge, wisdom, feedback, and kindness of the following individuals who have enhanced this book in countless ways: my Teachers College crew and dear friends Monisha Bajaj, Pete Cronin, Ameena Gaffar-Kucher, Mary Mendenhall, Kate Menken, Milagros Nores, Cambria Dodd Russell, and Moira Wilkinson; my CCNY colleagues Jesús Fraga, Amita Gupta, and Edwin Lamboy; my current and former CCNY students Maryam Dilakian, Pedro Guzmán, and Adalberto Muñoz; my friends Angela Paredes, Dina Goldstein Silverman, and Rob Sullivan; immigration lawyers Dan Diaz, Annie Wang, and Allan Wernick; my uncle David Mozeshtam, aunt Doris Shlayn, and sister Beth Vayshenker. Finally, I want to acknowledge all the immigrants who generously shared their stories and whose diversity, courage, and heart continue to strengthen the United States.

History, Demography, and Terminology

AN OVERVIEW OF THE BOOK

The United States is often referred to as a nation built by immigrants. However, its history with immigration has not always been a welcoming one, especially for certain groups. This uneven approach toward immigration has created a vital debate that has yet to be resolved within the country. This book aims to generate a discussion on immigration through the combination of factual information and real-life stories, experiences, and quotes from teenagers and young adults that both tell and show the ways in which immigration has played out in our nation. As the future of this diverse democratic society, teens from immigrant and U.S.-born backgrounds alike need access to accurate information and varied perspectives about immigration in order to make informed decisions about our nation's future. That is the goal of this book.

You will find that the book is divided into twelve chapters that together present the topic of immigration from personal, historical, political, and international perspectives. Chapters 1 through 3 provide an overview of the nation's history with immigration, define relevant terms, provide recent statistical and demographic information, reveal the diverse reasons and ways immigrants make the journey to the United States, and uncover myths about immigrants. Chapters 4 through 5 focus on three significant and often misunderstood subgroups of immigrants: undocumented immigrants, refugees, and asylees. Chapters 6 through 8 move into an exploration of the varied struggles immigrants experience when living in the United States,

"Immigration is our history and it is our destiny."
—Marcelo Suárez-Orozco[1]

including racism, learning English, and managing/reconciling competing identities. Chapters 9 and 10 delve into the national debate on immigration as well as related laws and policies that either support or hinder immigration. Chapters 11 and 12 analyze how immigrants become Americans, look beyond U.S. borders to reveal how other countries approach the challenges of immigration, and consider possible paths to move forward.

Within this book you will hear the real-life stories, experiences, and perspectives of teenagers and young adults who fit into all of the immigrant subgroups mentioned in this chapter. They are diverse in terms of where they came from, why they came here, how they came here, and how they feel about all the complex issues related to immigration. Some of the teens were featured in media articles or books; others were either interviewed by myself or members of a research team with which I have worked. Of those we interviewed, some (in collaboration with their parents or guardians) have given permission for their real first names to be used. Others will be referred to by pseudonyms, or made-up names, to protect their identity. What matters most are not the names of the individuals, but the powerful words they use to share their immigration realities.

A HISTORICAL PERSPECTIVE

For the overwhelming majority of people in the United States, immigration is either a recent reality or a distant memory that can be traced back to prior generations. The exception is Native Americans, people who have lived on U.S. land throughout time and are generally not considered to be immigrants or descendants of immigrants.[2] When Christopher Columbus landed on the island called Hispaniola, there were already anywhere from 2 to 10 million Native Americans in the hemisphere. This European intrusion began the unstoppable worldwide migration to this land and the eventual formation of the United States of America. Currently, the United States receives more voluntary immigrants than any other nation in the world. In spite of its history, "the United States is still wrestling with its own historical identity as a nation of immigrants."[3]

Four major waves, or periods, of immigration define the key time frames that different groups from various regions made their way to the United States. The first immigration wave began in the 1600s during the colonial period, a time when there were no laws or regulations regarding who could enter this region or even become a citizen. The second wave, which began around the 1820s, saw the start of immigration rules and regulations as 10 million immigrants from northern and western Europe came to the country to escape religious conflicts. The third wave began in the 1880s as policies of exclusion of certain groups were enforced and two world wars spurred global migration movements. The fourth wave started in the 1960s, when the United States began strict enforcement of immigration laws, and continues to this day. Each wave is characterized by large numbers of immigrants from specific parts of the world who experienced *push* factors in their home countries that set them on a path of searching for a better life. These factors range from religious to economic to social issues that negatively impact their lives and contribute to the life-changing and oftentimes difficult decision to relocate to a new nation. On the other hand, *pull* factors are those reasons that bring people to the United States or any other nation. They include the religious, economic, and social freedoms as well as opportunities that do not exist for them back home, such as jobs, education, and a better overall quality of life. Table 1.1 outlines each wave of immigration with the most prominent countries or regions people came from, the push factors happening in that part of the world, and the situation in the United States at the time. See if your family's history can be traced back to one of the nation's immigration waves.

THE PROCESS

The act of moving across international borders is a life-changing one. When people move from one country to another for a period of time beyond just a short-term visit, this is referred to as immigration. *Immigration* is the act of moving *to* a new nation. *Emigration* is the process of moving *from* one's country of origin.

Table 1.1. Immigration Waves to the United States

Wave	Approximate Time Period	Key Countries/ Regions of Origin	Reason for Emigration/ Push Factors	U.S. Context/ Pull Factors
1st	1600–1820	England Netherlands Scandinavian nations African nations	Religious persecution Trading, economic opportunity Religious repression Brought to the United States (and other nations) for slave labor	◎ No immigration regulations ◎ United States inhabited by Native Americans ◎ Formation of U.S. colonies
2nd	1820–1880	Germany Ireland China	Failed German revolution, poor economy, crop failure Great Potato Famine, starvation Limited economic opportunities	◎ Discovery of gold in California ◎ Free land plots to all settlers in the West for five years of development ◎ Availability of jobs in railroad ◎ Growth of steel and oil industries
3rd	1880–1960	Norway, Sweden, Denmark, Finland, and Iceland Italy Philippines Japan Mexico Eastern Europe Armenia Cuba	Regional wars and agricultural problems Internal conflict, violence, poverty, diseases Educational opportunities, Philippines is granted independence Rapid industrialization left many jobless, especially in agriculture Revolution and Bracero Program Fleeing anti-Semitism Escaping massacres in Turkey Political refugees	◎ Completion of Civil War ◎ Need for cheap labor following slavery ◎ Labor shortages due to World War II

		Origin	Reason	Notable Events
4th	1965–Present	Dominican Republic	Natural disasters, economic struggles	◉ Civil rights era
		Haiti	Government corruption, lack of economic opportunities	◉ Rise in service-oriented jobs
		Mexico	Lack of employment opportunities, family reunification	◉ Increased immigration regulations after 9/11
		India and China	Promise of education and technical jobs	
		Bosnia	Refugees escaping civil war and persecution	
		Central America (El Salvador and Guatemala)	Refugees escaping civil war	
		South America (Colombia and Venezuela)	Escaping civil war and political persecution	
		Middle East (Iran, Iraq, and Afghanistan)	Refugees escaping war	

INVOLUNTARY IMMIGRATION

Most immigrants came to the United States because it was a choice they made; it may not have been an easy choice, but it was nonetheless their own. However, not everyone who came to this nation had a say in the matter. Some immigrants came to the United States unwillingly or by force; these groups were brought here through colonization, conquest, and slavery.[4] As opposed to those who volunteered to make this life-changing transition, these groups are considered involuntary immigrants due to the way in which they ended up in the United States, through the imposition of others.

African slaves are rarely thought of as immigrants, but that is exactly what they were from the sixteenth to the nineteenth century. Africans from countries such as Nigeria, Ghana, and Senegal were brought to the United States (many also went to South America and the Caribbean) in slave ships to provide their free labor for White plantation owners and others who exploited them. Their most basic human rights were denied. While most immigrants came to a new country to start a better life, African slaves experienced just the opposite situation. Their freedoms were stripped away as they were forced to work extremely hard, but earned nearly nothing for their labor.

For the African American descendants of slaves in the United States, their immigration history is a hazy one. The histories of their ancestors, including the nations from which they emigrated and languages they spoke, have been erased. Unlike second-, third-, and fourth-generation Europeans in the United States who have at least a general sense of their family's country(-ies) of origin, many African Americans do not have access to information about their ancestors beyond the large and diverse continent from which they were brought over as slaves and involuntary immigrants.

The difference between these terms is whether the focus is on the country where one will be living or the country from which one is leaving. We can say that physicist and Nobel Prize winner Albert Einstein emigrated from Germany and pop star Rihanna immigrated to the United States at the age of sixteen. However, there are exceptions to this definition when we consider Puerto Rico, Guam, and the U.S. Virgin Islands. These U.S. territories are required to follow the rules and regulations of the U.S. government, and their land and surrounding bodies of water are also controlled by the United States. When we take away the requirement of crossing international borders, the process is then called *migration*. People migrate when they move to a new town, city, or state within their country. Regardless of whether one moves halfway across the world or from a city to a suburb, the process of immigrating or migrating brings many challenges and opportunities.

THE CASE OF PUERTO RICANS

Puerto Rico is an island in the northeastern Caribbean Sea. It became a territory of the United States in 1898, and in 1952 it became a commonwealth of the United States. This gave the island a political status unlike that of any other independent nation. It has its own autonomous government, its own constitution, and Puerto Ricans speak a different language (Spanish), but the United States has the right to make decisions about Puerto Rico's foreign affairs, trading goods and services, and political status, among other areas. For Puerto Ricans, this has been the single most controversial issue related to its national political identity.

Since 1917, anyone born on the island automatically has U.S. citizenship. As a result, Puerto Ricans can freely travel between both nations and live in either place. Although Puerto Ricans cross international borders when they come to the United States, they are not classified as immigrants due to their nation's territorial status.

Puerto Ricans are not technically considered immigrants in the United States, but they are often perceived as such because they come to this country faced with many of the same challenges as people who emigrate from other nations, such as learning a new culture, learning a new language, and finding ways to make a living. In 2007 there were over 4 million Puerto Ricans living in the continental United States, compared to almost nearly 3.9 million living on the island, making them the second largest Latino subgroup, following Mexicans.[5]

When the conversation turns to immigration, Puerto Ricans have been left out of the dialogue. This means the issues and problems they encounter in the United States have largely become invisible because as a group they do not fit within the immigrant label. Do you think Puerto Ricans should be considered immigrants in the United States? In order to include this group in the dialogue, Jason Irizarry, a New York Puerto Rican (who are often referred to as Nuyoricans), has begun writing about the process of crossing borders as (im)migration.[6] The placement of parentheses allows for the inclusion and validation of all migration experiences, whether it be across states, territories, or nations.

THE PEOPLE

There is a wide range of terms used to describe people who go through the process of leaving their home country for a new nation. Most commonly they are referred to as *immigrants* or *foreign born*. Both of these terms can be applied to people born outside of the United States. Since there are many differences regarding how, why, and under what circumstances people immigrate, there are also subcategories that further describe or label their situations. Currently, immigrants without legal status have fewer opportunities, face discrimination, and are often treated poorly. *Status* refers to whether an immigrant has official permission from the U.S. government to live, work, study, and/or visit the country and to remain in the United States when their period of authorization expires. Immigrants are referred to as "out of status" when they enter the country without permission or if the condition under which they were granted permission to be in the United States is no longer valid. For example, if a person receives a work visa and no longer works for the company that sponsored him or her, or if the individual is issued a student visa and remains in the United States beyond the completion of his or her studies without requesting and being granted an extension, that person becomes out of status.

There are many ways to describe people living in the United States without governmental authorization. They include *undocumented immigrant*, *unauthorized immigrant*, *illegal immigrant*, *unlawful immigrant*, and *illegal alien*. Although all these terms refer to the same group of people, some terms have strong and negative value judgments attached to them.

There are also a variety of terms and categories for immigrants who live in the United States with authorization. Immigrants who have permission to permanently live in the United States are allowed to do so for reasons such as having family members who are citizens, employment opportunities, or visa lotteries that they have won in their home countries. These people are called *lawful permanent residents* (LPRs). The government provides LPRs with a *permanent resident card* (often referred to as a "green card") that allows them to live and work in the United States as well as travel internationally. Once someone is granted LPR status and has lived in the country for five continuous years, he or she has the choice to apply to become a citizen. In order to become a citizen, a person must first pass a citizenship exam to become a *naturalized citizen*. Once an immigrant holds citizenship status, he or she is qualified for all the rights and privileges of U.S.-born citizens. The only exception is that a naturalized citizen cannot become president of the United States. However, he or she can hold any other government position at the federal, state, and local levels.

Nonimmigrants are individuals who are permitted to reside in the United States for a defined period on a temporary visa, often to work or study in the country. A *visa* is a document stamped into a foreign passport by the U.S. government; it grants permission to a citizen of a different country to be in the United States for a specific reason and/or time period. People who fit into this group include international students, visitors in the country for pleasure or business, and temporary workers. Migrant workers, who often work in agriculture moving across the country based on the availability of seasonal jobs, fit into this category. If a nonimmigrant overstays the time restriction stated on the visa, his or her status could change to undocumented.

While sometimes left out of the immigration discussion, there are two smaller groups of migrants with very specific experiences that have allowed them to reside in the United States. *Refugees* are individuals who have lived through severe persecution or discrimination in their home country and have been granted special permission by the U.S. government to come to America. In addition to being given a legal status, refugees also get additional privileges and support in their transition to starting a new chapter of their lives in a different country. Like refugees, *asylum seekers* have also experienced persecution in their country of origin. However, unlike refugees, who receive permission to enter the United States from their home country or the country where they were last living, asylum seekers are already living in the United States, often without permission, and are seeking asylum status from the U.S. government so they can legally reside in this country. If they are granted asylum, they become *asylees*. The ability to get refugee or asylee status depends not only on the treatment one received in their home country but also on the relationship the United States holds with that nation (see chapter 5 for further information). Figure 1.1 shows the percentages of each immigrant subgroup living in the United States in 2008. Figure 1.2 presents the states where the majority of immigrants lived in the same year.

Although immigrants technically must be born outside of the country where they are living to fit within this label, there are individuals who fall within a gray area. One such group are *transnationals*, people who are born in the United States but spend a great deal of time, often during their childhood, in

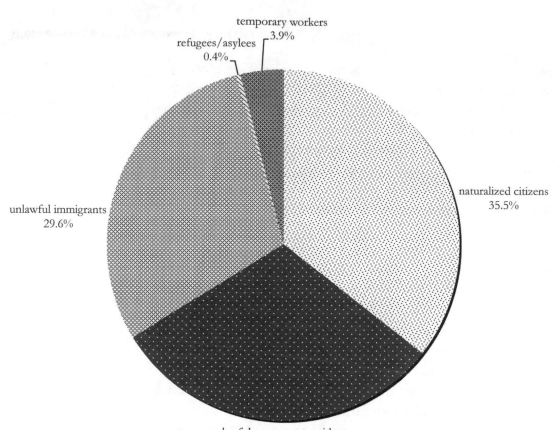

Figure 1.1.   Immigrant subgroups in the United States in 2008[7]

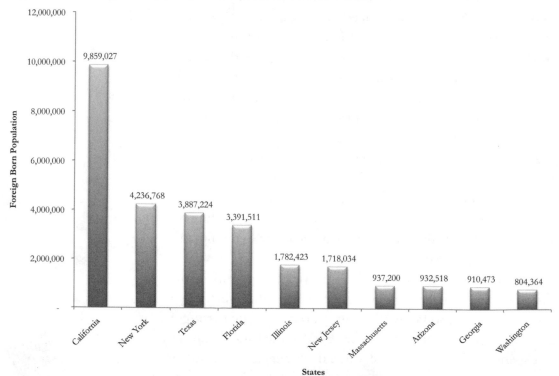

Figure 1.2.   States with highest immigrant populations in 2008[8]

A WARNING ABOUT TERMINOLOGY

In order to describe and categorize people we often need labels. While labels are created for practical purposes, they are also used as a way to rank certain groups and discriminate against them. For example, throughout U.S. history, there has been a range of terms used to describe those of African descent (Black, Negro, Colored, etc.). All of these terms have not been equal in the way they describe the group. Therefore, it is up to each person to decide which words to use and which to reject, especially because the terms we select hold both explicit and hidden meanings. The same can be said of the plethora of terms used to describe undocumented immigrants. Think about the images that come to mind when you hear the words *illegal* and *alien*. This book avoids the term *illegal immigrant* because an immigrant's legal status is not the same as the immigrant as a person; that is, a person cannot be illegal, so it would not make sense to refer to an illegal immigrant. We also avoid the term *alien*, which conjures images of an uncomfortable foreignness, and in fact is often used to talk about extraterrestrials. The terms *illegal* and *alien* will be used only to refer to the language used in specific policies or documents, or in quotes where people have used these labels. You will also notice that within this book the choice has been made to use the terms *unauthorized* and *undocumented* interchangeably to describe immigrants who do not have U.S. government permission to be here. These decisions about the use of terminology are important, because words matter! The choice of words not only reflects political views and attitudes, but also contributes to the way we understand the things we talk about.

their family's country of origin. Therefore, even though they were born in America and are U.S. citizens, they grow up or are raised in a different country, culture, and language. When they return to the United States, they often have experiences that mirror those of new immigrants, in spite of their status. A second group that also fits into a gray area are people who have experiences that are just the opposite of transnationals. *Generation 1.5* is the term used to refer to people who immigrated with their families to the United States at a young age. They often spend the majority of their childhood in the United States and are very familiar with the American culture and the English language, so much so that they often do not speak their family's native language. Although they are referred to as immigrants, their experiences are similar to U.S.-born citizens. The term *1.5* is used to describe their situation because it differentiates these individuals from first-generation immigrants, who came to the United States later in life, and second-generation immigrants, who were born in the country to immigrant parents.

TRANSNATIONAL HIGH SCHOOL STUDENTS

In New York City it is common for students with families from the Dominican Republic (DR) to grow up between the two countries during their childhood and adolescence. This back-and-forth movement can happen for a number of reasons: extended family members help raise children while the parents work long hours in the United States; the length of time it takes to receive visas; changes in the parents' marital or financial status; children are sent to the DR to "straighten up" or to attend better schools. Here are three transnational high school students speaking about their experiences living and going to school between two nations:

Luca

Luca is a high school junior. He was born in the United States and lived there through first grade. He completed second and third grades in the DR, fourth and fifth grades in New York City, and sixth, seventh, and eighth grades back in the DR; from ninth grade on, he has attended high school in the United States. Luca explains, "It was kind of hard; it was difficult. I mean, some things are in Spanish but . . . that's what I hate about my situation—that I went to DR and forgot English. Not entirely, but most of the basic stuff. But yeah, it was difficult."

David

David is a high school senior whose frequent back-and-forth experiences from a very young age has led to such a complicated history that even answering straightforward questions about his life has become tricky (interviewer's voice is indicated in italics):

> *Where were you born?*
> I was born in the Dominican Republic.
> *Uh-huh.*
> Not really. I was born here, but I was raised in the Dominican Republic.
> *Okay, so you were born in New York City. And then you were raised in the DR. So when did you go to the DR?*
> That was actually kind of a crazy experience. I studied one year here, I went back to the DR for a year, then I came back again for one year, and I went again for eight years. I came back when I was a freshman.

Tiara

Tiara is a tenth grader whose time between the United States and DR has created challenges in terms of school work:

> There are changes that I have from going back and forth, like being in DR, then coming over here. . . just when I'm getting used to class being all in English, then I go back over there and it all in Spanish.
> *How are the Regents [state high school graduation exams] for you?*
> Here it's more difficult because of the questions. . . . It's like that since I have been going back and forth and studying here and studying over there. Like the History Regents—it's difficult 'cuz with the history over there, I know it more than here. And then I come here, and I'm studying the history but I don't get everything, you know? Like there's my head; it's crazy sometimes. I was telling my teacher I wish the Regents was about DR, that way I would pass it [laughs].[9]

The life of a transnational individual can create a double-immigration experience in both countries as these students have to become (re)acquainted with the language, culture, and academics particular to each location. However, there are positive aspects to transnational upbringings, such as maintaining contact with family in both countries, being bilingual and bicultural, and understanding the realities of two very different places.

THE NATION OF IMMIGRATION

While immigration is often thought of as a phenomenon that happens at extremely high rates, on a global scale only about 3 percent of the world's citizens are immigrants.[10] That equates to about 191 million people. Therefore, the overwhelming majority of people in the world remain in their country of origin. However, if we were to place all the world's immigrants into one "nation of immigration," that country would be in the top five most populated nations in the world.

RELATED RESOURCES

Books

Encyclopedia of American Immigration, edited by Carl L. Bankston III (Pasadena, CA: Salem Press, 2010)—A comprehensive overview of U.S. immigration geared toward high school and college students. The 525 essays are written to address essential immigration questions/topics.

The African Americans: *Major American Immigration*, by Richard Bowen (Broomall, PA: Mason Crest Publishers, 2008)—This book provides a historical overview of African immigration to the United States. It begins from the slave trade and moves into recent migration. Issues of equality and treatment are weaved into the book.

Website

The Statue of Liberty-Ellis Island Foundation, www.ellisisland
.org/—This interactive website allows users to search the
passenger database of immigrants who may have passed
through Ellis Island. It also has a feature where individuals
can trace their family history or genealogy.

NOTES

1. Beth Potier, "City Leaders, University Unite to Improve Local
Education: Harvard Hosts Cambridge Elected Officials and Senior
Managers," *Harvard Gazette*, March 13, 2003, www.news.harvard.
edu/gazette/2003/03.13/15-cambridge.html (accessed October 19,
2008).

2. Contradictory views regarding the origin of Native Americans
in the United States still exist today. There are theories that the group
came from what is currently Siberia and Asia some twelve thousand to
thirty thousand years ago. However, evidence has been found to show
that Native Americans have always been in what is now the United
States.

3. Walter A. Ewing, "Opportunity and Exclusion: A Brief History
of US Immigration Policy," Immigration Policy Center, November
25, 2008, p. 7, www.immigrationpolicy.org/sites/default/files/docs/
OpportunityExclusion11-25-08.pdf (accessed October 16, 2010).

4. John Ogbu and Herbert D. Simons, "Voluntary and
Involuntary Minorities: A Cultural-Ecological Theory of School
Performance with Some Implications for Education," *Anthropology
and Education Quarterly* 29, no. 2 (1998), pp. 158–188.

5. Pew Hispanic Center, "Hispanics of Puerto Rican Origin
in the United States, 2007," July 13, 2009, pewhispanic.org/files/
factsheets/48.pdf (accessed January 13, 2010).

6. Jason G. Irizarry and René Antrop-González, "RicanStructing
the Discourse and Promoting School Success: Extending a Theory
of Culturally Responsive Pedagogy for Diasporicans," *CENTRO
Journal* 19, no. 2 (2007), pp. 37–59.

7. Jeffrey S. Passel and D'vera Cohen, "A Portrait of Unauthorized
Immigrants in the United States," Pew Hispanic Center, April 14,
2009, pewhispanic.org/files/reports/107.pdf (accessed February 8,
2010).

8. Migration Policy Institute, "Percent Foreign Born by State (1990, 2000, 2008)," MPI Data Hub, www.migrationinformation. org/datahub/acscensus.cfm (accessed April 7, 2010).

9. Kate Menken, Tatyana Kleyn, and Nabin Chae, "Meeting the Long-Term Needs of English Language Learners in High School" (report to the New York City Department of Education), 2007, pp. 11–12.

10. Philip Martin and Gottfried Zürcher, "Managing Migration: The Global Challenge," *Population Bulletin* 63, no. 1 (2008), www. prb.org/Publications/PopulationBulletins/2008/managingmigration. aspx (accessed March 3, 2009).

2   **Immigration Stories**

There are millions of immigrants from every part of the globe living in the United States. Each person has a story that vividly shows the struggles, successes, and emotions that make up the immigrant experience. Although statistics can provide a general overview of who our immigrants are and where they come from, they do not give us an in-depth perspective of the immigration experience. It is the individual stories of immigrants that allow us a window from which to see and understand what they experienced as decisions were made to leave their country of birth, make the voyage to the United States, and settle into a new country, culture, and language. This chapter contains the stories of five immigrants who came to the United States as (pre)teens or young adults. Each immigrant shares, in her or his own words, both the positive and negative realities of leaving one nation behind and starting a new life in another.

RITHA, HAITI

Reasons for Leaving

I came to the U.S. with my dad and my big brother in 2005. I was twelve. My aunt, uncle, and cousins, who we now live with, were already here. I had to leave behind my mom, two siblings, and most of my mom's side of the family in Port-au-Prince.[1] It was really sad because I had always lived with my mother and I had to leave her to come here. I was really close with my siblings too. One day I will bring my mom here by

Figure 2.1.   Map of Haiti

working hard and achieving my goals. It's really hard to keep in touch with her because she doesn't have a cell phone. I only get the opportunity to talk to her once or twice a month. I am happy that I came here. My cousins are really great and so is my dad, but I am still sad and miss my mom because before coming here I'd been with her for so long. I am more used to my mom than my dad, so it's just hard.

We came here for many reasons. In Haiti there were always kidnappings; there was a lot of bad stuff going on in Haiti. They killed young kids going to school; there were times it got so dangerous that students couldn't go to school. So we decided to come here for me to have a better education. That was the purpose and the goal and for my dad to have a better job—just to have a good life. Here my dad is a car salesperson. My dad and I had been talking about coming to the U.S. for so long. And then one day he decided, "Tomorrow we're going to apply for permission." We were working on the papers, like working on getting the visa. My dad went to get it [the visa] to see if we could come, and when he told me we were given permission, he was really surprised. After we found out, I had to move out from my mom's house to go live with him to do paperwork. I was really excited because I heard many people talking about the U.S. My cousins who were already here would tell us, "Oh there is money, you can work, and you can be anything you want to be. You just have to try hard." I was like, "I want to go there; maybe I can help my mom have a better life." Now that I live here I see that you can achieve many goals in the U.S. if you work hard; that's true. But some things, like there's money falling from trees, are not true. The difference is in Haiti you think the United States is like paradise. People think that everybody here has money and there is no poverty. But as soon as you get there you realize that you just have to work to get your money. It's not really like that, and there is some bad stuff here too. Everywhere has its negative aspects.

The Journey

My dad and I took the plane here because we are residents. There's this saying in Haiti: once you get into the plane it's like the cemetery. It means when you get on the plane, there's no coming out. So I was scared, really scared. But once we landed and I saw the buildings, I was really excited to begin a new life. Our uncle came to pick us up from the airport. Since it was the middle of winter, our family actually sent clothes for us so when we came we'd have coats to wear when we arrived. My first thought when we started driving away from the airport was, "Wow, it's really different from Haiti." The buildings looked different and the people on the street did too. The way of dressing in the winter was so strange to me.

A New Beginning

The biggest challenge being here was getting used to being in a new country and getting comfortable with learning English—getting confidence and speaking it without people laughing at you. I have a strong accent actually. When people hear me speak they think, "She has an accent; she wasn't born here." I know that I have to be comfortable speaking English. Confidence comes from seeing people like you trying, and when you see people trying, you think, "If I want to do this I have to try too." If you can't speak English you can't get good jobs, so you really have to try.

I started to go to a junior high school when I came here, and that's where I really focused on English. I had a good ESL [English as a Second Language] teacher who helped me a lot. I met friends that spoke my native language, and I was helping them and they helped me too. We were all learning English together, so it was kind of nice, but at the same time, you're finding trouble with other kids because you don't speak English and they speak English, and you're wondering if they are talking about you. Sometimes you get into fights because you don't want other people saying bad things about your country.

Now I go to a high school where all the students are immigrants and it's really different. I just feel safer. I just feel more comfortable being surrounded by people that I can be myself with, and the teachers are helpful. It's just like being in a place where you can learn English, and at the same time you can still use your languages and learn about new cultures. I have friends from Poland, Dominican Republic, and Russia. And while you're friends with them, you're learning their language and culture. I like that; it's really nice.

Figure 2.2.   Map of Russia

DINA, RUSSIA

Reasons for Leaving

I came to the United States when I was almost thirteen with my parents and grandparents in 1992. The primary reason we left Moscow was anti-Semitism.[2] Our windows were knocked out for putting a menorah[3] on the windowsill during Hanukkah. There were also limits to how far one could rise in their professional career due to being Jewish. My parents were also fairly active in the dissident community, and they were persecuted for that as well. The final reason was economic, as with my family's education, we believed that we could make a better life in the United States.

The Journey

The process of coming over involved a lot of standing in lines at the immigration office, asking for political refuge at the American Embassy, and being invited by someone who was a first-degree relative—my mother's uncle had immigrated and sent us an official request. Then we had to interview with the CIA [Central Intelligence Agency] and the embassy to be approved, and once we were granted religious and political refugee status, we had to start shipping our belongings over and go through medical exams. It was an extremely lengthy process that involved a lot of bribing of Russian officials.

We sold a lot of our belongings. The hardest part was giving away our books. My family had a huge library, hundreds of books on shelves all around our apartment, and we could only bring a few. My grandmother had to sell some of her heirlooms that she had gotten from her parents because there were certain pieces of silver or china that were considered national antique properties and couldn't legally be brought out of Russia. For some reason, I was told to iron towels and sheets for packing. I think my parents thought that if you iron something, it would pack easier and fit better, so I did a lot of ironing and lot of washing of dishes. I wanted to be very mature and grown-up and help. We had to get rid of literally everything—our apartment was stripped bare, down to the kitchen cabinets that someone bought and ripped off our walls. It was like watching your whole life taken down, plank by plank.

We traveled by a chartered plane that had been booked by the Hebrew Immigrant Aid Society. We were packed in with a ton of other immigrants after hours of waiting, going through the final humiliating customs inspection, saying goodbye, perhaps forever, to people that dropped us off at the airport. I remember seeing all these people trying to hug each other one more time across the dividers—you had to say good-bye before going through customs, and officials were trying to hurry things along. It was literally a swarm of people, yelling, crying, very emotional, grabbing at their elderly and their children and their belongings. Once we were on the plane, I became airsick and slept through most of the flight and vomited a lot—now, I think that it was just stress, and my body was reacting to it. When we landed in the U.S., I remember it was a beautiful sunny morning, and everyone started cheering and clapping once the flight attendant made the announcement.

A New Beginning

I didn't expect it to be easy to adjust, but I expected a place where everyone is free, where people can be what they want to be if they are willing to work hard, where I could get an education regardless of my faith. My parents instilled those expectations in me—they always believed that we would be okay in the end, even when things got tough.

When we got to Texas, and I remember thinking that it was very hot—it was September, which in Texas is the height of summer. I also remember thinking that it was very clean, very bright, and very new. I remember having my first glass of orange juice and thinking how sweet it was.

I expected that there would be struggles, but I always knew that we'd be okay in the end. My parents had a hard time finding jobs at first, and I always worried about money. . . . I still constantly worry about money, and I think it comes from growing up in Russia and then immigrating and never having enough. At school, adjusting was tough initially, but by high school, I had made lots of friends, joined clubs, started playing soccer on the high school team, and I was very content.

What surprised me about Texas was how many churches were everywhere and blonde people, and how ignorant everyone seemed to be of world events. The evening news was all about local events, and nobody at school seemed interested in what was happening in the Middle East or Europe. Everyone was worried about the Dallas Cowboys winning the Super Bowl. I remember thinking how closed-minded everyone was.

My life has definitely changed due to our immigration experience. I wouldn't have been able to get a Ph.D. if we had stayed in Russia, or if I did, it would have been much more difficult. We have freedom; we don't have to be afraid at night, and we have been able to achieve professionally and financially.

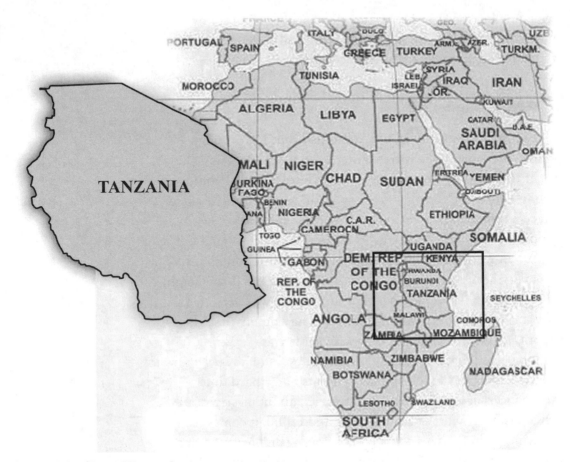

Figure 2.3. Map of Tanzania

ALDA, TANZANIA

Reasons for Leaving

In 2004, when I was seventeen years old, I came to the U.S. with my mother. We joined my father and other members of my family, who had already been living in the country for a little while. My dad had a job and that's why we came. He worked with the United Nations [UN] in the ministry of foreign affairs in Tanzania and was transferred to work in New York. Since I was in my last year of high school when we learned about the move, it was decided that my mother would stay in Tanzania with me until I graduated.

When I first heard that my family was going to be relocated, I was not really happy, because you realize you're going to be in a new group. It's like when people go to college out of state; I was also going away after finishing high school, except it was out of the country. I was very sad because I knew that I'd probably never see most of my friends and it is true; I have not seen them in six years. I kept talking to those who are my best friends, who are very close, dear to me, but you really don't have time to stay in touch with everybody. But after some time of thinking about how my life could change for the better, I started to feel really excited, actually, to come here.

The Journey

When you are coming to America for a job, it is very different than somebody who is applying to come here on a student visa, where you have to follow more complicated procedures. I was a minor, so I just went with my dad to take a passport picture and get fingerprints, which was it. It was not a big process, no interviews. After I graduated high school, my mom and I left. The trip felt like my first time in a plane—although I had traveled when I was younger, I did not remember it—so I was a little bit scared. But I made it.

A New Beginning

New York was not as exciting as I thought it would be because you see these pictures of just the city and buildings, and it's not like that everywhere. Where I lived everything was really quiet. It was not as exciting as I imagined. I thought, "Whoa, this is it?" It was as if I had moved to the countryside kind of feeling.

In Tanzania we really do not experience the cold. Since my mother and I traveled in January, it was right in the middle of winter. It was also my first time to see snow. We did not own jackets. I just wanted to be inside to avoid the freezing cold. I noticed that the neighborhoods were very clean. The first few months because I did not leave Long Island, that's all I knew about the United States. I had not yet seen the city [New York City]. I was stuck in this house in the middle of winter because nobody really wanted to give you a tour in the winter. So, I actually waited until May or June to see the city.

I had planned to start college right away, but that didn't work out because of the grading system in my country. Also, my test scores were not ready to apply for the fall. I missed the deadline so I had to wait a whole year without school and that was a little bit boring for me. My expectations were a little bit crushed from the system. When my grades and my SAT[4] scores finally came in, then I was able to apply and I started attending a community college. A major difference in the educational system was that in Tanzania, the path you took in high school is the same major you take in college. You have to decide what you want to be really early on. But here it's different; you can major in international studies as an undergrad and be a teacher for grad school. When I first started, I majored in business administration, but it was not something I enjoyed. I took it because my dad had advised me to do so, and since I was in a new country, I felt like I didn't really know what would be best for me. So I followed his suggestion. I was in it for three semesters until I decided to transfer to a four-year college where I could focus on a liberal arts major. I chose to be an international studies major and am in my senior year.

Since I've been here I've started to let go of some Tanzanian traditions. When my parents were here [after Alda's dad retired from his job at the UN, most of the family returned to Tanzania], we used to go to the embassy and if it was Independence Day there would be a party, but not any more. I even forget that December 9 is my country's independence day. Once I saw somebody's Facebook status that said, "Happy Birthday, Happy Independence Day Tanzania." I was like, "Oh yeah, it is the 9th of December."

I am graduating next year. I am planning to get a job here in the United States because I get a work permit for a year and hopefully the company I work for will sponsor me for a green card. I am just being positive about it. I want to be hired by the United Nations too. But I want to work in Africa; that is my overall goal.

Figure 2.4.   Map of Honduras

AMILCAR, HONDURAS

Reasons for Leaving

   I came in the year 2005 when I was twenty-three years old. I decided to come from my small town of Bajamar, Honduras, leaving behind my mom, sisters, brothers, and dad. I came to look for another opportunity to live because in my community I could not find a way of life. Poverty is a factor that impacted us the most. I saw my mom selling coconuts in the city and that affected me. It was very painful in my heart because I wanted to help her economically, so she would not have to go through those situations in life, but at the same time I could not because there are no jobs in Honduras. I had to look for another way of life, to find money, and the path was to come to the U.S.

I decided to make the journey with a friend who had tried to cross before. I asked him if I could come with him. He asked me, "Do you have your ticket money?" I told him I only had two hundred dollars. He said, "No problem, let's go. I'll show you the road." We left with a small group of young guys from our community on a journey that lasted two months.

When I thought about coming, I did not have hope to come in an airplane because I did not have papers. So, the only way was to risk my life by taking busses and the train, and then walking across the border from Mexico to the U.S. I left carrying a backpack and a sweater, which helped me, but at the same time I thought to myself that God never knew what the cold was. We had always dealt with risks. In my town we dealt with the ocean, the mountains, and the animals, but this risk was extreme. The trip to the U.S. on the train was about being careful, I believe, and having the physical condition to endure everything that happens on this kind of trip: rain, sun, cold, and many other obstacles.

The Journey

First, I took the bus from the town of Bajamar to Puerto Cotes in Honduras. Then, I took another bus to the border of Honduras and Guatemala, then another to the capital of Guatemala, and from there a bus to the border of Guatemala to the Mexican city of Hidalgo. From there the trip on the train began. We call those freight trains "the black beast" or "the steel snake." When I saw the way I was going to come to the U.S., hanging from a train for days and nights, I said, "God, if this is the way I'm going to get to the U.S., protect me and take care of me because I will get on that train anyway." The first day when I saw it I was scared. I thought, "God, I was not expecting this." There is only one train that leaves every day. So I missed the train that day because I was too afraid to hold on to it. I was afraid that I would not hold on tight enough and that the train would cut off a leg or my head. Every day we missed a train would be more spending money and not moving ahead. When the train came the next day at approximately four in the morning, the train beeped and beeped and it was coming at a very high speed. I said, "God help me." I ran at the train's pace for like a minute to give me some time to decide whether to take it or not. In the end I took it, and from there another part of my journey began.

To go through Mexico, through the whole country, for a Black person is not easy. We were a group of six Garífuna guys who could be seen from far away. It was an experience that is not only about racism; it is simply that you are Black in a Ladino[5] community so everyone wonders who you are, where you come from, because in Mexico there aren't people who look like us. We had to hide from the authorities. We could not take the bus because people would instantly know that we were not from there and that we were immigrants or they could come up with other ideas about us. Then to go through all that is Mexico City, there were several obstacles you have to overcome. It's not easy to evade Mexico's police and immigration patrol as we also tried to avoid thieves and rapists along the way.

A New Beginning

Thank God I had the opportunity to get here. Now I see the change in my life because I have a job. Now, I don't have to wear the same shirt for two or three years. Now, I can buy myself a shirt and give some money to my mom and to my dad. When they receive this money, they are really happy because they can buy the provisions for the house, food, and continue living in a community that's pretty, but where it is challenging to live without a good home, proper nourishment, and a good education.

When I got here I felt a difference in the air the day I started to work. That was a great happiness for me because my dreams were starting to become a reality. I wanted to find a job to help myself and to help my family; that was one of my goals. I saw that everything was changing and I was happy. I am still happy.

I had a friend that had an apartment and an old bed who helped me a lot. He let me live with him for seven months. After I paid my $2,500 debt to the coyotes[6] I was able to find a room to rent. I paid rent every fifteen days; thanks to my job I was able to do so. Another friend who knew a contractor found me a cleaning job. I cleaned offices, swept the yard of buildings, and picked up the garbage. I have always found good people, nice bosses, too.

I believe that not having documents is one of the biggest disadvantages because people take advantage of you. You do jobs that should be better paid, but they do not pay you that because they say, "If you want to do it, you do not have documents so I can't pay you more for that job."

My plans are to see my daughter grow here as an American and work hard until God allows it. I would like to go back to my country, to see my family and come back, but I can't say that I would go back to my country to live; that would be impossible. I believe my life is America already.

KAWEENA, CHINA

Reasons for Leaving (Returning and Leaving Again)

My mother left Beijing, China, to come to the U.S. by herself in 1989. Her migration was due to the combination of a bad marriage and the opportunity to work at a software research company. Two years later, when I was six years old, I made the journey to Pennsylvania with my father so that we could join my mother. At that time I was too young to understand what it meant to live in a different country away from the rest of my family, but I was just glad to see my mom again after our extended separation. I was also excited about living in a country that had Disney World!

After two years in the U.S. I melted into the American culture within a short period of time and was comfortable within my environment. At the same time, when I was eight years old, my mother decided to send me back to China because her company gave her an opportunity to work in Hong Kong

Figure 2.5.   Map of China

for a short period of time and she wanted me to maintain and improve my Chinese before returning to the U.S. for good. Since her job involved a lot of travel, she thought it was best for me to live with my grandparents in Changchun, the northeast region of China. That way I wouldn't have to spend most of my childhood traveling on an airplane. It turned out that returning to China was actually more of a cultural shock for me than coming to the U.S. the first time around.

Following five years of living with my grandparents, I was told I hadn't been obedient enough and that my grandma had a rough time controlling my "untamed nature." I was getting in trouble at school from time to time for not behaving and being too much of a tomboy. According to Chinese tradition I was expected to act like a well-brought-up girl by doing well in school and being obedient.

In 1997 at the age of twelve I returned to the U.S. The decision made by my parents was that I would return to the U.S. to complete my education. This second time back, the impact was much greater on me. I knew it would be difficult for me to stay in contact the friends that I'd made during my five years in elementary school in China. I also felt that everything I learned to become familiar with fitting in the Chinese culture was done in vain. Many times I felt that I immigrated to China and was then returning to the U.S. instead.

The Journey

Both times, I flew to the U.S. The flights were very long, somewhere around fourteen hours, and going through customs made the experience even longer. I remember when my mom sent me back to China, that time I went by myself. I was placed in first class, and I thought that was pretty fun.

A New (and Second) Beginning

When I first arrived to the U.S. late at night I saw it as lifeless, silent, and scary. However, when I woke up the next morning there was so much green outside my window in Philadelphia. Also, the sight of a sunny playground definitely changed my mind about America. For a six-year-old, it didn't take much to be impressed. When I returned as nearly a teenager, I definitely noticed that the air that filled my lungs was much more fresh and crisp than the polluted air I was accustomed to breathing in Beijing. At the same time, I thought there were too many lights around at night, as if everyone were scared of the dark. Still, the streets were not as busy and bustling as any in China. The second time around I certainly felt more calm than scared, as I had been the first time.

The first thing I realized when I went to junior high school was that teachers did not hit, give physical punishments, or have strict discipline! In China I had to stand for an hour two different times without lunch for being rowdy in class. I felt like I was the best behaved kid in class from all the strict guidelines we had to follow in China, such as sitting with our hands behind our backs so we couldn't play with whatever was in front of us.

The most difficult part about immigrating was learning and relearning the language. I remember when I came back to the

States the second time, my English wasn't as good as it used to be, and making friends right away was difficult. Looking back now, I find it funny that the White, Black, Jewish, and Hispanic kids in my class all became friendly with me pretty quickly and were willing to help whenever I needed. As strange as this may sound, some of the Asian kids who were born in America did not really want to speak with me at all. It wasn't until my English improved and I became somewhat popular that their attitudes toward me changed. I began to notice that the American-born Chinese students would rarely associate themselves with "FOBs"—fresh off the boats—as they mockingly called Chinese people who just arrived to America and didn't speak much English. Regardless of what they thought of me, I continued to dedicate much of my early teenage years to perfecting my speaking and writing skills and focusing on getting into a good high school and eventually college.

The best part of the immigration experience for me was being thrown into a completely new environment and having the chance to observe the differences between my native and the new culture. I was able to gain a lot of insight just by observing these differences as well as similarities. I believe many immigrants who are able to succeed recognize the differences, accept them, and capitalize on their ability to integrate the best ingredients from multiple cultures to create new hybrid ideas, services, and ways of thinking that intrigue people from all backgrounds.

QUESTIONS FOR REFLECTION

Consider each of these immigrant stories, as well as those of people you may know or perhaps your own, to answer the following questions:

- What did you learn from the immigrant stories presented here (and others you may be aware of)? What were the major similarities and differences?
- What are some of the reasons people decide to leave their country of origin?

⊚ **What are the different challenges one might experience coming to the United States as a child, teenager, and young adult? Is there an age at which it might be easier or more difficult to make such a life change?**

⊚ **How does immigration affect family structures? In what ways are families reunited and separated?**

⊚ **What are the greatest challenges for newly arrived immigrants? What are the surprises they face as they get to know their new surroundings?**

Immigrants currently reside across the states, cities, and towns that make up the United States. If you are an immigrant, speak to people who came from a different part of the world to learn about the reasons they left their country, how they came to the United States, and their experience adjusting to a new land. If you were born in the United States, seek out people in your community who are immigrants to learn about their migration process. It is through the details of people's stories that we can come to better understand the complex decisions, emotions, and realities of the many immigrants who make the United States their new home.

RELATED RESOURCES

Books

First Crossing: Stories about Teen Immigrants, by Donald R. Gallo (Cambridge, MA: Candlewick Press, 2007)—This book is a compilation of the stories of ten teen immigrants from across the globe. There is a focus on their varied experiences and struggles.

Kids Like Me: Voices of the Immigrant Experience, by Judith M. Blohm and Terri Lapinsky (Boston, MA: Intercultural Press, 2006)—This book presents the stories of immigrants from the age of ten to their mid-twenties. Students from Mexico to Moldova share their experiences of moving to a new land.

Websites

My Immigration Story.com, www.myimmigrantionstory
.com—This website offers a range of stories from recent
immigrants via photographs, video clips, audio recordings,
and written accounts. Immigrants are invited to share their
own experiences and stories on this interactive site.

Independent Lens: The New Americans, PBS.org: www.pbs.
org/independentlens/newamericans/—This website shows
the real-life stories of immigrants from different parts of
the world. For example, the stories of Ogoni refugees from
Africa, Dominican baseball players, and Indian technical
workers are told. They share how they came to the
United States, what they do for a living, their dreams and
challenges, as well as the art, music, food, and languages
from their nations.

NOTES

1. The earthquake that hit the city of Port-au-Prince in 2010
destroyed Ritha's mother's house. While her mother survived, two of
her teenage cousins were killed.

2. Anti-Semitism is the discrimination and hatred toward Jewish
people.

3. A menorah is a nine-branched candleholder used by Jews
during the eight-day celebration of Hanukkah, which commemorates
the triumph of the Maccabees in rededicating the Holy Temple in
Jerusalem and the miracle of the oil burning for eight days.

4. The SAT (Scholastic Achievement Test) is a standardized test,
which includes sections on mathematics, writing, and reading. It is a
requirement for admissions into certain colleges.

5. In some Central American countries, including Honduras,
people of mixed indigenous and Spanish background are referred to
as Ladinos. This is not to be confused with the language of Sephardic
Jews, which goes by the same name.

6. *Coyote* is a term used to refer to individuals who are paid by
undocumented immigrants to smuggle them across the U.S.-Mexican
border. See chapter 9 for additional information.

Immigration Myths and Realities

There are many outlets of information about immigrants in the United States. News outlets such as television, radio, magazines, and newspapers provide a range of views about immigration, as do less traditional media such as blogs, YouTube videos, and websites. While these sources provide a wide range of information, they may also present false or misleading ideas that lead to myths and other misinformation. Therefore, it is important to check that the sources have a solid reputation and stay in line with the facts. With the seemingly never-ending availability of information, it is more important than ever to be critical of where it comes from and how it is presented.

How informed are you about current issues regarding immigration? Take this short quiz to see what you already know and what you may need to learn more about. See which statements are true and which ones you think are false. You may even want to discuss why you feel that way about the statements and on what information you've based your decisions.

1. **Immigrants are taking American jobs.**
2. **Immigrants today are less successful than those from earlier generations.**
3. **Immigrants come to the United States and resist learning English.**
4. **Immigrants commit a lot of crimes.**
5. **Nearly all undocumented immigrants come from Mexico.**

6. **Undocumented immigrants do not pay taxes and take advantage of government services.**

7. **If undocumented immigrants just make the effort, they could change their status.**

How do you think you did? If you answered false for all seven statements, you are correct! Each of these statements is based on a myth about immigrants in the United States. Certain media outlets and some individuals spread these false ideas, either because they themselves are misinformed or because they want to develop fear of or discrimination against immigrant groups. Below you'll find a section on each of the seven myths. Each begins with a range of quotes from mostly U.S.-born teens regarding their take on these issues. Let's look more carefully at these statements to separate fact from fiction.

MYTH 1: IMMIGRANTS ARE TAKING AMERICAN JOBS.

"These immigrants are taking our jobs. Due to the fact that they don't pay taxes, they are costing us money. Also, America is expected to adapt to these immigrants when it should be the other way around."
—Laura, United States, 17 years old

"They are taking the jobs that poor U.S. citizens could have."
—Berta, United States, 17 years old

"If immigrants are willing to work twice as hard for the same pay, why not let them work here."
—Pete, United States, 19 years old

"They come to this country to work hard. They work harder than Americans."
—Nathan, United States, 18 years old

At times when the economy is not doing well and people are losing their jobs, immigrants are easy targets to blame. However, the reality is much more complicated. Immigrants often come to the United States because of the availability of jobs for them. These jobs primarily exist at two levels of the economic system. First, there are the low-skill, low-wage jobs such as those in agriculture, construction, and domestic services that lure immigrants, who are paid significantly below minimum wage and often work under poor and unsafe conditions for long hours. However, undocumented immigrants tolerate these jobs mostly because the pay is much higher than in their home countries, and they can send money back home to help support their families there. Second, there are jobs that require specific skills that American workers may lack. These jobs can be found in areas of technology, engineering, and the sciences. The U.S. government actually has specific visas called H-1B to allow professionals from these fields to acquire documentation to temporarily emigrate for up to six years from their homeland (although it is possible to get an extension). If these jobs, at both ends of the economic ladder, were not available or were already taken by American citizens, many immigrants would not change their life situations to come to the United States. Figure 3.1 shows the ten most common jobs held by immigrants working in the United States.

BRAIN DRAIN

The United States often welcomes immigrants who are highly educated. Professionals tend to leave their country when they do not have opportunities in their field, are poorly paid for their skills, or reside in nations with unstable and dangerous governments. The U.S. government has special visas to allow those with expertise in areas such as science, engineering, and technology to live and work in the country. While their presence benefits the United States, it is a significant loss to their countries of origin. Many developing nations desperately need the skills of these individuals to improve their country. This phenomenon of educated people leaving their homes to seek better opportunities and quality of life is referred to as "brain drain." Nations that have experienced brain drain include the former Soviet Union, Ethiopia, and Iran, among many other countries from all over the world.

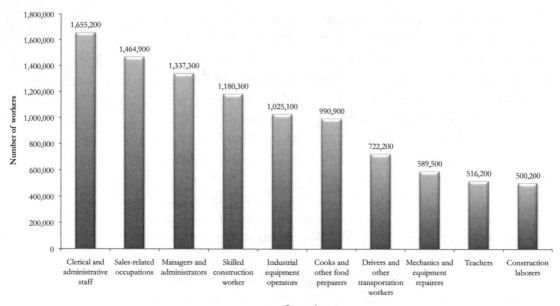

Figure 3.1. Top immigrant occupations in the United States[1]

The concept of American jobs is one that needs to be examined. Over time our economy has become increasingly global. That means that although we live at the local level—that is, in cities, towns, or communities in the United States—the products we consume are created all over the world. You may be using a pen made in France, wearing shoes made in Honduras, and watching a television made in China, although the company that sells these products may be American. This is due to the availability of cheap labor in those countries, where there may be fewer labor laws or safety regulations.

MYTH 2: IMMIGRANTS TODAY ARE LESS SUCCESSFUL THAN THOSE FROM EARLIER GENERATIONS.

"I don't see that immigrants are doing that well or really even helping our country."
—Conner, United States, 17 years old

The countries from which immigrants arrive in the United States have varied throughout history. But what has remained constant is that immigrants have been looked down upon due to their foreign ways, limited formal education, and minimal English skills. Immigration has almost always been perceived as a threat to U.S. society, American culture, and the English language. This fear has remained consistent throughout the four waves of immigration the nation has experienced (see chapter 1), but has grown recently due to the increased racial and ethnic diversity of the newest Latino and East Asian immigrants.

TAKING A LOOK AT WORKING CONDITIONS

When American companies hire undocumented immigrant workers, they may take advantage of the immigrants' status by overlooking poor or unsafe working conditions. This creates unfair conditions for the immigrants as well as U.S. citizens and indicates that immigrants are not the cause of the lack of employment opportunities in the United States. The solution lies in the creation and enforcement of rules and regulations to create safe work environments, fair pay scales, and changes to a broken immigration system that would instead allow humane opportunities for all workers. Until such changes occur we can say that "increasing inequality created demand for immigrant workers and thus spurred immigration."[2]

While it may appear that immigrants from prior generations were more successful, we must keep in mind that the jobs and skills required for them were also different. For example, during the European immigration waves, factory and industry work was readily available and English skills were not required for such positions. Nowadays we are in an era where most workers are required to have more developed skills, education levels, and English proficiency. However, there is still work in construction, agriculture, and in the service sector where such skills are not required, but the pay is significantly lower as well. In spite of the challenges immigrants face in coming to a new country, over time they have been able to integrate into American society through improving their English skills, purchasing homes, and, when possible, becoming naturalized citizens.[3] To truly see the success of immigrants, regardless of when they arrived in this country, we must look to the second and third generations, who consistently have more education, higher paying jobs, and more developed English language skills than their parents and grandparents.[4] A recent study that looked at three generations

ACKNOWLEDGING IMMIGRANTS

The Carnegie Corporation of New York, named after the famed Scottish immigrant, businessman, and philanthropist Andrew Carnegie, highlights immigrants from all over the world who have made a difference in the country through their diverse contributions. Every year the corporation puts out a publication around the nation's Independence Day (July 4th) called "Immigrants: The Pride of America."[6] The following are a sampling of immigrants acknowledged for their successes in the United States in 2010:

- Wayne Gretzky, hockey legend from Canada
- Djimon Hounsou, actor from Benin
- Charles Kao, Nobel Prize winner in physics from China
- Feniosky Peña-Mora, dean of Columbia University School of Engineering from the Dominican Republic
- Anna Wintour, editor-in-chief of American *Vogue* from England

of Mexicans living in the United States found that their education progress across generations was equal to or greater than that of European immigrants from the late nineteenth and early twentieth centuries.[5] Success of immigrant groups cannot and should not be judged solely based on the achievements of first-generation newcomers.

MYTH 3: IMMIGRANTS COME TO THE UNITED STATES AND RESIST LEARNING ENGLISH.

"Learn our language or go home!"
—Maria, United States, 18 years old

"It's wrong when people who can speak English speak their language IN AMERICA. And there shouldn't be an option to 'press 2' for Spanish."
—Kurt, United States, 16 years old

Anyone who has ever traveled to a foreign country knows that communicating in a new language is a difficult task. Living in a country where one does not speak the language involves constant challenging tasks, from sending a package at the post office to filling out forms to asking directions. Aside from individuals immigrating to the United States who are fortunate enough to learn English in their country of birth or come from a country where English is spoken, many immigrants arrive with minimal English skills. Learning any language takes a great deal of time and effort. It can take anywhere from three to seven years, with proper instruction, to reach a level where you can speak as well as read and write at a high level.[7] However, most immigrants are expected to immediately speak English, and only English, after only a brief period in the United States. To make matters more difficult, many adult immigrants face significant challenges when it comes to learning English in a school setting. While there are places that offer English as a Second Language (ESL) classes, they are either overbooked with waiting lists that may require immigrants to wait for years for a space to open up, or they are costly and out of reach of immigrants who may not have the resources to attend such courses.[8] Also, some immigrants hold down multiple jobs, leaving them without the time to take courses.

Most immigrants do learn some English, but their children or grandchildren generally learn only English, losing the valuable resource of their native language and complicating their ability to speak with previous generations of their own family.[9] Children of second and third generation immigrants often find themselves in college wishing they had not resisted learning their family's native language and begin taking classes to connect with their heritage and to communicate with older members of their family.

If it appears that immigrants do not learn English, this is only because of the consistent arrival of new immigrants who only speak their native language(s). Immigrants understand that English is the language of power in the United States and it is a key to success for themselves and their children.[10] The greater challenge may be in convincing Americans that the goal for everyone should not just be speaking English, but being multilingual in order to truly be a part of the shrinking global world we all share.

MYTH 4: IMMIGRANTS COMMIT A LOT OF CRIMES.

"Illegal immigrants should be put in jail, because that's treason."

—Frank, United States, 17 years old

"They [undocumented immigrants] are spies and terrorists in the American eye. Can't we just shoot them?"

—Jeremy, United States, 16 years old

43

"Immigrants are people just like you and me. Just because they want to have better lives doesn't mean they are horrible people. We are all in America due to immigration!"

—Anna, United States, 16 years old

A common misconception about immigrants is that they commit crimes at high rates. The media contributes to this stereotype, especially in the way and rate at which Latinos are represented in the news. One study found that over a three-week span, the local news in Orlando, Florida, showed Latinos as "criminal suspects" 28 percent of the time, which was two times higher than African Americans and over five times more than the portrayal of White people.[11] While many Hispanics are U.S.-born citizens, many people simply assume all Latinos are foreign born (as is often assumed for Asians too). This misconception plays into the immigrant as criminal idea. The reality is that immigrants are actually less likely than U.S.-born individuals to commit crimes. The percentage of men between eighteen and thirty-nine years old who are in prison is 3.5 percent for those born in the United States and only 0.7 percent for immigrants. This means that male immigrants are five times less likely to end up in the prison system than U.S.-born men. Similarly, the criminal levels for Mexican-, Salvadoran-, and Guatemalan-born individuals, who make up the majority of the undocumented immigrant population, were just as low.[12] In fact, researchers found a correlation between states with the highest rate of immigrants and the lowest rate of crime.[13] That means states with more immigrants actually have lower crime rates than states with fewer immigrants!

Another reason for the false belief that immigrants commit crimes is because those who are out of status are labeled as "illegal." There are many people in the country who commit crimes, large and small, yet they do not have to live on a daily basis with that label, the way many immigrants do. According to our legal system, coming into the country without authorization, or "entering without inspection," is a misdemeanor that is punishable with a maximum sentence of six months in jail and a fine. Immigrants who come to the United States with a visa and stay beyond the deadline have committed a civil infraction, which is categorized as a violation. A violation differs from a crime (such as a misdemeanor) in that it has less severe penalties such as lowered fees and little to no jail time. However, all undocumented immigrants can also be deported to their home country.

When we think of acts associated with those who "break the law," we generally think of violent crimes such as murder, robbery, or rape. But living and working in a country without authorization is a different type of behavior, which does not involve hurting others in the way that criminals often do. Nevertheless, when immigrants make the choice to cross the border without documentation, according to the U.S. government they are breaking the law. Many unauthorized immigrants have few options when it comes to following immigration laws, though they would like nothing more (see myth 7). Undocumented immigrants are put in a position of being criminals simply because of who they are, regardless of what they are doing.[14] A person who shoplifts or drives over the speed limit has committed a crime. This is so regardless of background because anyone who steals or speeds could suffer consequences of the law. However, border crossing is only a crime for a specific group of individuals. In other words, there are people who cross land, water, and air borders on a daily basis, but only some are punished or categorized as criminals for doing so.

Looking back through laws that have been enacted in the United States reveals imperfect and unjust legislation. For example, at different times of the nation's history it has been legal to keep people as slaves, to give citizenship only to White people, and to limit voting rights to men. These laws have been changed over time to create a more fair system for people of different backgrounds. Immigration laws may also be changed in the future so that they do not discriminate against certain groups and do not categorize immigrants as criminals.

MYTH 5: NEARLY ALL UNDOCUMENTED IMMIGRANTS COME FROM MEXICO.

"When I think of undocumented immigrants I think of Mexicans."
—Omar, United States, 19 years old

"Many American Filipinos do not realize that the undocumented exist within their community and that many of them need help in breaking the stigmas attached to their legal status."
—John, Philippines, UCLA Undergrad[15]

Most people think of Mexicans when the topic of illegal immigration comes up. However, the United States is home to undocumented immigrants from all over the world. Currently there are approximately 7 million undocumented Mexicans in the United States out of the total of 11.9 million, which means that the Mexicans account for 59 percent of undocumented immigrants in the United States.[16] Another 17 percent of undocumented immigrants are Latinos from other Latin American nations. The proximity of the United States to these countries and their poor economic situation help explain why so many Mexican and other Latin American nationals make their way to the United States in search of better opportunities for themselves and their families. Outside of Mexico and Central and South America, approximately 11 percent are from Asia, 4 percent from the Caribbean, and less than 2 percent come from the Middle East.[17] Although these are the largest groups, undocumented immigrants come to the United States from every region of the world. The countries of origin of undocumented immigrants living in the United States in 2008 are shown in figure 3.2.

MYTH 6: UNDOCUMENTED IMMIGRANTS DO NOT PAY TAXES AND TAKE ADVANTAGE OF GOVERNMENT SERVICES.

"If you want to live in America you have to be American. You have to pay taxes and speak English and most illegal immigrants don't do that."
—Janine, United States, 16 years old

"I don't care if life is hard where you came from. You come to this country, don't pay taxes, and make more trouble for America."
—Alvin, United States, 16 years old

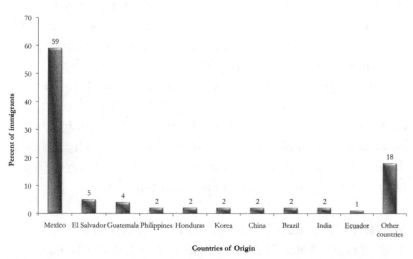

Figure 3.2.   Top countries of origin of undocumented immigrants[18]

While many believe that undocumented immigrants take more than they give when it comes to paying taxes, the reality is just the opposite. Studies have found that they actually pay more into the government system than they use. In other words, undocumented immigrants use fewer services relative to what they pay in taxes compared to U.S. citizens.[19] Undocumented immigrants pay taxes in a variety of ways. Any time they purchase an item or pay for their housing, they are providing local, state, or national tax dollars. Although about a quarter of undocumented immigrants have jobs in the informal sector that pay them "under the table," the majority (75 percent) pay taxes that are deducted, or taken out, of their paychecks. Undocumented immigrants whose wages are taxed may be the result of them getting jobs in the formal sector and using a taxpayer identification number (TIN) or providing false social security numbers, which is a crime in and of itself. As a result, undocumented workers paid approximately $7 billion into the Social Security system in one year, in spite of the fact that they do not benefit from most of these funds.[20]

Tax dollars generally go toward government services such as financial support for people who are unemployed, food stamps, and housing assistance, all of which undocumented immigrants are not eligible to receive. There are two primary sources of services that unauthorized immigrants do obtain though tax dollars: K–12 public education for their children and emergency medical services. In some cases out-of-status immigrants are wary of using these services for fear of their status being revealed and the risk of deportation. Therefore, generally speaking, undocumented immigrants pay into a system for which they receive only minimal benefits. According to one study in Texas in 2006, undocumented immigrants paid $1.58 billion of state taxes, yet only used $1.16 billion of services.[21] This means that undocumented immigrants in many states actually help, rather than hurt, the economy, not only through the labor they provide, but also directly through tax dollars they pay.

MYTH 7: IF UNDOCUMENTED IMMIGRANTS JUST MAKE THE EFFORT, THEY COULD CHANGE THEIR STATUS.

"Illegal immigrants should be deported because you can register and be legal if you want to stay in the United States."

—Zack, United States, 16 years old

"We should send them back and have them work hard to come here legally."

—Jerry, United States, 17 years old

"My family worked hard to get into this country and people are just sneaking in; it's not right."

—Agata, United States, 18 years old

Most immigrants who are here without documents are eager to change their status and would do whatever it takes to become permanent residents or citizens. After all, many risked their lives in extremely unsafe conditions, trudging through deserts, holding onto boats, or being stuffed into the trunks of cars on their journey to the United States. Surely they would not object to further sacrifices in order to be able to live outside of the shadows. The problem is that it is nearly impossible for most people who are labeled "illegal aliens" to change their status.

The decision to enter the United States with or without papers starts in one's home country. There it is possible to apply for over fifty different types of visas to lawfully enter the United States. They range from visas for people who would just like to visit the country, to student visas to attend U.S. colleges or even high schools, to temporary or permanent work visas. While all these options may sound hopeful, the reality is rather bleak. First, the wait to have an application reviewed and to receive an answer can take up to twenty years. Second, the application fees can be very expensive. For example, in Mexico the fee for a visa application comes to about $130, which can be nearly a month's salary for a minimum-wage worker.[22] Lastly, the chances of being granted a visa are very slim, as strict limits are placed on the number of people accepted from specific countries and based on the types of visa. Also, visas may be denied based on other factors one cannot control, such as the decisions of the people who work at the consulate. In the 1990s, Brazilian workers noted that when applicants looked "poor or rough," they were rejected, based on these biased and often racist criteria.[23] While this was later found to be illegal, such biased practices still exist. Recently, a twenty-five-year-old Peruvian woman was accepted to study for a master's program at a U.S. college but was then told by the consulate worker that her request was being denied because "she was still young."

Once a person resides in the United States without legal status, there are few avenues through which one can get documents. It used to be the case that an individual could change status by marrying a U.S. citizen in a male-female marriage. Gay or lesbian couples never had this option. However, it has become increasingly more difficult for individuals who entered without documents to use marriage as a way to earn lawful permanent resident (LPR) status. There are an increasing number of mixed-status families, where husbands, wives, and children have a combination of unauthorized, LPR, and citizen statuses. For example, 40 percent of immigrant families in California had such a reality, as did 20 percent in New York and 10 percent across the nation.[24] While an undocumented immigrant may have a child born in the United States who is automatically an American citizen, there is a false belief that the child's parents will be granted citizenship as well. However, this approach does not allow for parents to change their status because a child must be at least twenty-one years of age before he or she can sponsor a parent to become a legal resident. Once an immigrant is out of status, or undocumented, on U.S. land, there is little that can be done to change this, aside from being sponsored by an employer, spouse, parent, or adult child. Few employers sponsor undocumented immigrants, as they risk admitting that they hired someone out of status, have to pay increased taxes and salaries, and must prove they could not find an equally qualified U.S. citizen or LPR to fill the position. Therefore, the greatest hope most undocumented immigrants currently have to attain legal status is through immigration reform or laws passed by the government. An example of this for teens and young adults is the DREAM Act (see chapter 10). If we look back in our history, a broader example of such a reform actually passed in 1986. It was called the Immigration Reform and Control Act, which created a path toward citizenship for anyone living in the United States without documentation since 1982. Until Congress creates changes to the broken immigration policies that we currently have, the outlook for undocumented immigrants who want to change their status is a dreary one.

Figure 3.3. An immigration march across the Brooklyn Bridge on March 31, 2006, in New York City to demand immigration reform that would provide rights to all immigrants. Photo courtesy of Pedro Guzmán.

While there are protests occurring throughout the nation against immigration, there are also marches and other events taking place in favor of the rights of immigrants, all immigrants.

"ANCHOR BABIES": THE TERM AND LEGISLATION

The label *anchor baby* has been used to describe children born in the United States to undocumented parents. It has been falsely believed that by having a child who is an American citizen, the parents will gain such a status too. The metaphor of an anchor is used to bring up images of being able to stay in one place; in this case the place is the United States. For some people the term *anchor baby* is a derogatory label to describe a child and his or her parents. However, Martin, a U.S. citizen born in California to undocumented immigrants, explains, "I use that term to identify myself, but I do not feel offended by it. I am proud to have hardworking parents that came here and tried to better themselves. The anti [immigration proponents] used the term to label us, but I do not feel offended."

In 2007 U.S. Representative Nathan Deal of Georgia proposed the Birthright Citizenship Act. The act aimed to reverse the Fourteenth Amendment of the Constitution, which automatically provides U.S. citizenship to anyone born in the country. This act proposed that children born to undocumented immigrant parents would no longer be granted U.S. citizenship. The bill was unsuccessful and did not become a law.[25]

ANTI-IMMIGRATION SIGNS

Immigration is an issue that people often have strong feelings about. Below are some slogans that represent anti-immigrant views from a website called Stop the Illegal Invasion.[26]

- Go Home and Fix Mexico
- Americans Wake Up!! Stop the Invasion!
- Taxpayers against Freeloaders
- No More Anchor Babies!
- Deportation? Si Se Puede! (Yes We Can!)
- No English? Know English!!
- Tired of Pressing "1" for English?
- Patriotism Is Not Racism

RELATED RESOURCES

Books

Gangs in Garden City: How Immigration, Segregation, and Youth Violence Are Changing America's Suburbs, by Sarah Garland (New York: Nation Books, 2009)—The book presents the story of former immigrant gang members in the suburban area of Long Island's Nassau County. The author shows, through individual stories, how the historical involvement of the United States in Central American nations connects with gang-related issues in the country.

"They Take Our Jobs!" and 20 Other Myths about Immigration, by Aviva Chomsky (Boston, MA: Beacon Press, 2007)—The author debunks immigration myths related to the economy, laws, race, and the debate in general.

NOTES

1. Matthew Bolch, Shan Carter, and Robert Gebeloff, "Immigrants and Jobs: Where U.S. Workers Come From," *New York Times*, April 7, 2009, www.nytimes.com/interactive/2009/04/07/us/20090407-immigration-country.html (accessed May 20, 2010).

2. Aviva Chomsky, *"They Take Our Jobs!" and 20 Other Myths about Immigration* (Boston, MA: Beacon Press, 2007), p. 13.

3. Gregory Rodriguez, "From Newcomers to New Americans: The Successful Integration of Immigrants into American Society," National Immigration Forum, 1999, http://www.ccis-ucsd.org/PUBLICATIONS.wrkg147.pdf (accessed November 2, 2009).

4. Kevin F. McCarthy and Georges Verenz, "Immigration in a Changing Economy: California's Experience—Questions and Answers," RAND, 1998, www.rand.org/pubs/monograph_reports/MR854.1/MR854.1.chap4.pdf (accessed December 10, 2009).

5. Nancy Foner and Richard Alba, "The Second Generation from the Last Great Wave of Immigration: Setting the Record Straight," *Migration Information Source*, October 2006, www.migrationinformation.org/Feature/display.cfm?ID=439 (accessed May 13, 2010).

6. Carnegie Corporation of New York, "Immigrants: The Pride of America," http://carnegie.org/programs/democracy-and-civic-integration/immigrants-the-pride-of-america/ (accessed October 20, 2010).

7. Jim Cummins, *Language, Power, and Pedagogy: Bilingual Children in the Crossfire* (Clevedon, UK: Multilingual Matters, 2000), pp. 57–85.

8. Chomsky, *"They Take Our Jobs!,"* p. 110.

9. Stanley Lieberson and Timothy J. Curry, "Language Shift in the United States: Some Demographic Clues," *International Migration Review* 5, no. 2 (Summer 1971), pp. 125–137.

10. Pew Hispanic Center, "Hispanic Attitudes toward Learning English," June 7, 2006, pewhispanic.org/files/factsheets/20.pdf (accessed December 29, 2009).

11. Ted Chiricos and Sarah Escholz, "The Racial and Ethnic Typification of Crime and Criminal Typification of Race and Ethnicity in Local Television News," *Journal of Research in Crime and Delinquency* 39, no. 4 (2002), pp. 400–420.

12. Rubén G. Rumbaut and Walter A. Ewing, "The Myth of Immigrant Criminality," Boarder Battles, May 23, 2007, borderbattles.ssrc.org/Rumbault_Ewing/ (accessed May 12, 2010).

13. Richard Nadler, "Immigration and the Wealth of States," Americas Majority Foundation, January 2008, www.amermaj.com/ImmigrationandWealth.pdf (accessed May 12, 2010).

14. Chomsky, *"They Take Our Jobs!,"* pp. 180–183.

15. John Carlo, "A Downward Spiral," in *Underground Undergrads: UCLA Undocumented Immigrant Students Speak Out*, ed. Gabriela Madera et al. (Los Angeles: UCLA Center for Labor Research and Education, 2008), pp. 29–34.

16. Jeffrey S. Passel and D'vera Cohen, "A Portrait of Unauthorized Immigrants in the United States," Pew Hispanic Center, 2009, pewhispanic.org/files/reports/107.pdf (accessed December 29, 2009).

17. Passel and Cohen, "A Portrait of Unauthorized Immigrants in the United States."

18. Michael Hoefer, Nancy Rytina, and Bryan C. Baker, "Estimates of Unauthorized Immigrant Population Residing in the United States: January 2008," U.S. Department of Homeland Security, February 2009, www.dhs.gov/xlibrary/assets/statistics/publications/ois_ill_pe_2008.pdf (accessed March 31, 2010).

19. Francine J. Lipman, "Taxing Undocumented Immigrations: Separate, Unequal and without Representation," *Harvard Latino*

Law Review 9 (2006), papers.ssrn.com/sol3/papers.cfm?abstract_id=881584 (accessed May 13, 2010).

20. Eduardo Porter, "Illegal Immigrants Are Bolstering Social Security with Billions," *New York Times*, April 5, 2005, www.nytimes.com/2005/04/05/business/05immigration.html?_r=1&scp=1&sq=Illegal%20Immigrants%20are%20Bolstering%20Social%20Security%20with%20Billions&st=cse (accessed December 4, 2009).

21. Carole Keeton Strayhorn, "Undocumented Immigrants in Texas: A Financial Analysis of the Impact to the State Budget and Economy," Texas Office of the Comptroller, 2006, www.window.state.tx.us/specialrpt/undocumented/undocumented.pdf (accessed November 25, 2009).

22. Embassy of the United States: Mexico, "Visa Services: How to Apply," www.usembassy-mexico.gov/eng/evisas.html (accessed December 29, 2009).

23. Philip Shenon, "Judge Denounces U.S. Visa Policies Based on Race or Looks," *New York Times*, January 23, 1998, www.nytimes.com/1998/01/23/world/judge-denounces-us-visa-policies-based-on-race-or-looks.html?pagewanted=1 (accessed November 18, 2009).

24. Michael E. Fix and Wendy Zimmerman, "All under One Roof: Mixed-Status Families in an Era of Reform," Urban Institute, October 6, 1999, www.urban.org/UploadedPDF/409100.pdf (accessed December 21, 2009).

25. H.R. 1490: Birthright Citizenship Act of 2007, April 19, 2008, www.govtrack.us/congress/bill.xpd?bill=h110–1940 (accessed April 17, 2010).

26. "Stop the Illegal Invasion," home.earthlink.net/~stoptheillegalinvasion/anti_illegal_immigration_signs.htm (accessed December 29, 2009).

Undocumented Immigrants

Poor, hard work, better future, Mexican, green card, suffer, sadness, innocent, money hungry, criminals, and deport—These are words that come to mind for U.S.-born teenagers in relation to the term *illegal immigrant*.

There are nearly 12 million immigrants in the United States who have never received permission to enter the country or who have expired visas. These immigrants—who are referred to as undocumented, unauthorized, or illegal—make up 4 percent of the nation's total population and 6.8 percent of students in kindergarten-through-twelfth-grade schools.[2] The difference between the number of unauthorized men and women is significant, with 6.3 million undocumented men and 4.1 million undocumented women in the country. Males between eighteen and thirty-nine years old make up the largest group. Many young men come to the United States to work and support families who remain in their home country.

One's immigration status is not a permanent or fixed state; for many people, it is something that changes over time due to their circumstances. There are two categories of unauthorized immigrants: entry without inspection (EWI) and visa violators. Migrants labeled as EWI usually enter U.S. borders by foot, plane, or boat. Most either come into the country using false documentation or sneak in by avoiding contact with border patrols. A smaller group includes those who are smuggled into the country to provide free or cheap labor or to become sex workers. Visa violators are those who stay in the United States after their visas expire, whether those visas be for tourism,

"I'm even afraid of eating an apple in the library because I'm afraid of getting caught."

—Mariana, Guatemala, undocumented college student, 23 years old[1]

work, or study in a university. Visa violators may also be those who do not follow the conditions for their visa. For example, a person here on a student visa who finds a job at the same time is violating his or her visa.

Nhu is an example of someone classified as a visa overstay. She emigrated from Vietnam with a student visa to pursue a business degree at the University of Colorado at Boulder. After graduation, she was employed by a company in Colorado that sponsored her for a work visa. After a year at the job, she grew to dislike her position and decided to leave the company. The day Nhu left her job, her work visa was no longer valid. She immediately went from being a temporary worker to an undocumented immigrant. All of a sudden her immigration status changed, and everything became infinitely harder.

MIXED-STATUS FAMILIES

It is becoming more and more common for a family to consist of some individuals who are undocumented immigrants and some who are U.S.-born citizens. This happens when undocumented parents come to America and have children, who automatically become U.S. citizens because they were born in the United States. In 2008 there were 4 million children born in the United States to undocumented immigrants. They make up 73 percent of the children whose parents are undocumented.[3] Mixed status not only exists between parents and children, but between siblings as well. Therefore, one or some of the siblings may be born in

---

DAILY ROUTINES OR DAILY CHALLENGES?

If you are a U.S. citizen or lawful permanent resident, there are things you do on a regular basis that are either difficult or impossible for undocumented immigrants to accomplish. Table 4.1 describes both government-related/ official and everyday/unofficial areas that are a constant source of difficulty for those who are unauthorized. Do you take any of the following areas for granted?

Table 4.1. Daily Routines or Daily Challenges?

Official/Government Challenges	Daily Life Challenges
◎ Have a driver's license	◎ Go to a nightclub that may ask for a driver's license or official U.S. government identification
◎ Drive, rent, or buy a car	
◎ Apply for public college fellowships, scholarships, and summer jobs	
	◎ Take an airplane to another state
◎ Apply for public student loans	◎ Purchase alcoholic beverages (when age twenty-one or older)
◎ Purchase a house	
◎ Enlist in the military	◎ Commit an infraction on public transportation or on the street, such as passing through subway cars while the train is in motion
◎ Travel to another country and return to the United States	
◎ Become certified to be a teacher, nurse, or doctor	◎ Report suspicious activity, a crime, or an assault to police
◎ Travel close to the border, where police stop people to ask for documentation	◎ Go to the airport to pick up/drop off someone
◎ Apply for a job that requires a Social Security number	◎ Go on a cruise
◎ Vote to elect city, state, and national officials	

another country while the younger children may be born in the United States.

A mixed-status family in New York City was featured in a *New York Times* series on immigration called "Remade in America." Both parents, along with their twenty-two-year-old daughter, Maya (a pseudonym), were born in Ecuador. Miguel, the seventeen-year-old younger brother, was born in the United States and is the family's only U.S. citizen. The differences between the two siblings are just as drastic as the difference in their immigration status. Maya was a top high school student who did not realize she was undocumented until meeting with her high school guidance counselor to complete college applications. After the counselor asked about her Social Security number, Maya asked her father, only to be told she didn't have one. In spite of this challenge, Maya went to a reputable public university in New York City, where she graduated with a degree in business and a 3.8 GPA (grade point average). She paid for college through babysitting jobs and the financial support of her father. After graduation, while

IMAGINE THIS

You come to the United States at the age of three with your family. You grow up like most children in your community, attending school, playing sports, and spending time with friends. Over time your connection to your home culture and language fades as you feel less like an immigrant and more and more American. English is by far your dominant language, and you only have a vague familiarity of holidays and foods common to your original culture. You grow up identifying as an American, but more importantly, as just "a regular kid."

Then one day you come home from a bike ride with your high school friends, and your mother warns you to be extremely careful. She strongly cautions you not to break even the most minor laws. For instance, she tells you to obey the street signs when you ride your bike, stay on the right side of the road, and make sure not to hang out with any kids who could get you in trouble. You try to calm your mom down and tell her not to worry. However, she tells you to sit down because she has something important to share with you. "I've decided that you are old enough to know the truth. You are illegal," she slowly mutters, looking down with shame and guilt. You look at her with confusion thinking, "What in the world is she talking about?"

It turns out your family came to the United States without documentation, and as a result you are an unauthorized or undocumented or, worse yet, illegal immigrant. In this instant your whole identity changes, and the person you thought you were is no more and now everything is centered on being illegal. Your life as you knew it, and expected it to turn out, changes. You must watch everything you do to avoid getting in trouble with the law so as not to end up being deported to a country that seems like a foreign land where people speak a language you barely remember. Also, you wonder about your future. Will you be able to go to college? How will you pay for it? And if you graduate, will you be able to find a job? Suddenly everything changes . . . imagine that.

her friends were applying to top-notch companies where they would earn salaries over seventy thousand dollars, Maya could not even consider such positions. She explains how her status determines everything that she can, and mostly cannot, do: "I used to think I was different [from other undocumented immigrants] because I went to college, but I'm no better than anyone else. Like them, I don't have my documents. So I'm just one among millions."[4] Maya did find a job working for a small company that serves immigrants who seek information regarding visas and immigration policy. She has a government taxpayer identification number that allows her to pay taxes on her salary but does not allow her to work legally. She has plans to return to college for a master's degree and is hoping the DREAM Act will pass (see chapter 10) so that her long-term plans can become a reality. In the meantime she makes the most out of a situation where she is treated like a second-class individual.

Miguel, her younger, U.S.-citizen brother, has different opportunities. He can (and does) travel to Ecuador to visit extended family, will be able to receive federal financial aid when he goes to college, and can live his day-to-day life without fear of being "found out" and deported. However, he does not seem to value these privileges and has even considered moving to Ecuador. His sister has taken him to advocacy meetings regarding immigration issues, but in spite of his being so closely connected to the plight of undocumented immigrants, he does not seem interested in the cause. Maya and Miguel may only have a five-year age difference, but in many ways their lives in New York City are worlds apart.

The differences between Maya and her father are also extreme, especially when it comes to the possibility of returning to Ecuador. Maya, who has lived in the United States since the age of fourteen, cannot imagine such a scenario. She explains, "All my friends are here. All I know is here. If I returned, I'd be lost." On the other hand, her father, who grew up in Ecuador but received a bachelor's degree in engineering in the United States while on a student visa, remains open to a return home. He says, "I crashed a party I was not invited to, and one day I'll be asked to leave. This is a place to work. Not to die."[5] Clearly, mixed-status families like this one differ not only by immigration status, but by generation as well.

CHOOSING BETWEEN SCHOOL AND WORK

The educational attainment, or years of schooling a student completes through high school and college, is lower for undocumented adolescents than for lawful immigrants and U.S.-born citizens. The most significant factor in the educational attainment of an unauthorized youth is their age of arrival to the United States. The younger the age of arrival, the more years of education they are likely to complete. Among undocumented immigrants who enter the country between the ages of fourteen and seventeen, only about half earn a high school diploma. By contrast, 72 percent of undocumented youth who arrive in the United States at the age of 13 or younger complete high school. The rates of undocumented immigrants attending and graduating from college are fairly low. In 2008 10 percent of undocumented individuals between the ages of twenty-five and sixty-four had taken some college courses and only 15 percent actually earned a bachelor's, master's, or doctorate degree.[6]

The statistics on high school graduation and college completion are important because there is a connection between educational attainment and income levels. A study by UNICEF (United Nations International Children's Emergency Fund) states that "education is perhaps a child's strongest barrier against poverty."[7] One reason undocumented immigrants hold jobs with lower salaries is due to their levels of schooling and lack of credentials, or degrees. In 2007 the average unauthorized immigrant family had a total income of $35,000 per year, whereas the average documented immigrant family made $41,300 and a U.S.-born household earned $50,000. Furthermore, adults who are undocumented are twice as likely to live below the poverty line than U.S.-born adults. Twenty percent of undocumented adults and 40 percent of undocumented children live below the federal poverty line, which in 2009 was $22,050 for a family of four and $37,010 for a family of eight.[8, 9] In the United States, as in most other countries, being poor not only creates daily challenges but also puts larger life opportunities out of reach for many. For instance, someone who lives in poverty is likely to have limited access to health care, attend poor-quality schools, and be exposed to higher rates of crime.[10] While growing up in poverty does not necessarily mean one will not have a comfortable life (including a good education, well-paying job, etc.), it certainly creates a range of obstacles in addition to those that undocumented immigrants already encounter. Figure 4.1 shows the most common types of jobs for undocumented immigrant workers in the United States.

Unaccompanied Youth on the Fast Track to Adulthood

While most immigrants under the age of eighteen voyage to the United States with immediate family members, there are a growing number of teens who migrate on their own. Some may have family already in the United States, but others set out alone without anyone to support them in this new and dangerous chapter in their lives. Unaccompanied teens are generally driven to come to the United States with two related goals in mind: to work and to support their family back home.

In Mexico youth stop attending school when they enter the workforce, and this marks them as adults (regardless of their age). Only 50 percent of Mexicans have completed the equivalent of a ninth-grade education. The other half have not studied beyond elementary school or have only completed a few grades of schooling. When unaccompanied Mexican youth under the age

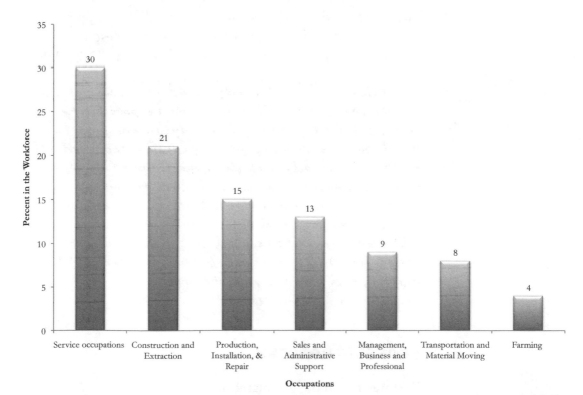

Figure 4.1. Top occupations for undocumented immigrants[11]

of eighteen come to the United States, many do not even consider education as an option. They believe that working is a better, or only, option for them in the United States, as they already see themselves as adults. Two teens still living in Mexico explain why they are planning to immigrate to the United States:

"Well . . . I would immigrate to go to work, because if I was going to study, it would be better to just stay here in Mexico."

—Saúl, Mexico, 16 years old[12]

"It [immigration] would be to make money, not to go study. Rather, one emigrates to become an adult, not to stay in adolescence."

—Judith, Mexico, 16 years old[13]

Being an adult to these young people involves working, and the responsibilities and pressures that come with it are intensified for those who are undocumented. Armando made the journey to the United States on his own and describes how, in spite of being seventeen years old, he is very much an adult:

"I think that I am already an adult because of the weight that I have, because of the responsibility. Well, I have to pay my own way, no one pays for me. I have to help my parents [in Mexico], and all of that. I already consider myself an adult, even though I am not of age. . . . I have to buy my own clothes, mmm, my rent, the light bill, food, all of that . . . things I did not do in Mexico. . . . I felt like a child over there. And here I don't because the responsibility is on me. I have to watch out for myself, and also for my parents."

Armando, Mexico, 17 years old[14]

CROSSING BORDERS

We often talk about the migration process of people from Latin America as crossing "the" border, implying the U.S.–Mexican border. However, the reality for immigrants from South and Central American countries is that they must cross multiple borders. Each nation or border they pass through adds another layer of risk when it comes to being caught and deported. In fact most migrants do not understand what to expect when they finally do get to the United States–Mexico border, as surveillance (police, border patrol, etc.) and legal consequences are often more extreme than at other border crossings. Deepa Fernandes, a U.S. journalist, asked border crossers on the Mexican side of the border about their reasons for coming to the United States. Most responded that they were going to find work. When she questioned them about how they would be treated once they made it to the United States, few understood that by coming into the country without a visa they would automatically be treated as criminals if they were caught by the border patrol.[15] They did not understand that by seeking out work, which is a respectable act, they would simultaneously be committing a crime.

In addition to the harsh natural conditions that those coming to the United States encounter on their journey, they also deal with human obstacles. On top of hunger, heat, or cold and exhaustion, many are robbed, molested, raped, and verbally degraded as they walk toward the border. Coyotes, police, and individuals who seek out migrants along the way commit horrible actions and crimes against already desperate border crossers.

"Some men came out of nowhere and they assaulted my parents and me. They stole all our money, as well as our belongings. My mom and I were touched in our private parts, it was terrible. I remember very well that day."

—Candida, Mexico, 18 years old[16]

"I went through hunger, thirst and even desperation during this long journey. I had to confront one of the most difficult situations during my life: the desert. I walked without food and water. I walked the whole day and when my strength grew we found a river. That was a sign of God's existence."

—Anonymous, Ecuador, immigrated at 11 years old[17]

63

DRESS CODE

Many people who set out to cross the border by foot are not aware of the harsh conditions they will face. Extreme weather; difficult paths through bush, desert, and rivers; wild animal encounters; starvation; and thirst over days of walking are challenges for even the most prepared. Some migrants believe they only have a short walk ahead of them and want to enter the United States looking their best. Women may wear their finest high-heeled shoes, but end up leaving them behind on the path. Women's dress shoes can be found littered along the path as evidence of false presumptions, big dreams, and even bigger obstacles.

Figure 4.2.   Smuggler's Gulch is a canyon area on the border of San Diego, California, and Tijuana, Mexico. Photo courtesy of Drs. Wayne Cornelius and María Luisa Zúñiga.

"We walked about six hours, but along the same route in circles since the main guide was high on drugs and the other two coyotes were new and didn't know the way."

—Anonymous, Mexico[18]

Although anywhere from 500,000 to 1 million individuals make it across the U.S.-Mexican border each year, it is estimated that 20–25 percent of these migrants are apprehended annually.[19] This means they are stopped by the U.S. Border Patrol and arrested or sent back to Mexico. For many potential border crossers, being detained is a disappointment but does not stop them from trying again and again. After being caught in the United States and brought back across the Mexican border, fifteen-year-old José reflects on his attempt. He and his father were planning to work in construction and earn seventy-five dollars each per day. The same amount would have taken one month for them to earn in Mexico City. José explains the decision he made to cross with his father: "I was following my dream to earn enough money so my family would not be poor. I only wanted to work; if I could earn that money here in Mexico, I would not want to go to the U.S."[20]

UNDOCUMENTED, UNACCOMPANIED MINORS AND THE LAW

What happens when unauthorized immigrants under eighteen are discovered to be in the United States without papers? The answer to this question has changed over time. At one time undocumented minors who were charged with crimes, whether crossing the border without permission, driving without a license, or using or selling drugs, were placed in immigration detention facilities (which are basically prisons) where they were placed side by side with adults. They experienced harsh conditions, such as having to sleep on concrete floors, and were abused by other prisoners and guards. When immigrant advocates learned of the realities that underage immigrants

WHAT'S THE DIFFERENCE?

Many undocumented immigrants come to the United States from Mexico (and other nations) because of economic opportunities. Table 4.2 shows the large difference in typical weekly salaries across a range of jobs that undocumented workers take in the United States.

faced, they fought for changes within the immigrant detention system. A lawsuit won in 2001 required detention centers to be created specifically for detainees under eighteen years old, and ended the mixing of adults and minors.[21] Currently, undocumented, unaccompanied minors charged with a crime are placed in holding centers specifically for youth as they await a decision about their future in the United States. All minors wait an average of forty-five days before seeing an immigration judge who decides whether they will be deported to their home country or allowed to stay in the United States. If the minors have experienced some type of abusive and oppressive circumstances in their home country, they might be granted asylum in the United States. Usually extended family already living in the country are sought out to sponsor the youth who become asylees (see chapter 5).

Table 4.2. Jobs Chart

Profession	Typical Weekly Salary in a U.S. City	Typical Weekly Salary in Mexico
Carpenter	$400	$ 85
Construction worker	$450	$ 75
Mason	$700	$ 85
Painter	$500	$ 80
Bricklayer	$600	$ 85
Electrician	$600	$ 95
Babysitter	$450	$140
Kitchen help	$500	$ 50

IT'S NOT JUST LATINOS

While most people associate entering the United States without authorization primarily with land crossings by Latinos, the case of Yong Zheng shows the diversity among undocumented immigrants and the ways in which they come to the United States. Yong, who was fourteen years old at the time of his migration from China, was his parents' second child, which violated the nation's one-child-per-family law. Having Yong caused financial hardship to Yong's family, who had to pay extra fees and taxes for their second child. Following his mother's death, Yong's father contacted a human smuggler, referred to as a "snakehead," who arranged for his son to receive a false passport to come into the United States. These services included a sixty-thousand-dollar fee, which Yong's father promised the snakehead would be paid once Yong began working in the United States.

Upon arriving in Newark, New Jersey, Yong was caught by immigration authorities at the airport and spent one year in a Pennsylvania detention center. Traumatized and confused about his situation, Yong was able to work with a lawyer and was released to live with his uncle in Ohio. There he attended school and became a top student. However, a miscommunication with an immigration officer led to a situation where Yong missed a monthly check-in meeting. He was called in, arrested, and told he would be deported to China. At the airport Yong banged his head against a metal pillar and knocked himself unconscious. He proclaimed, "He was better off dying in the United States than coming back to China and putting everyone at risk." The snakehead was threatening his family, and Yong thought he too would be in danger of being tortured and murdered there. His condition left him unable to make the flight. He was placed in a Houston detention facility, where a team of lawyers worked to get Yong a green card so that he could remain in the United States.[22]

THE INVISIBLE PRISON

While America is often referred to as "the land of the free," the freedoms are not equally afforded to all individuals living in the nation. Jong-Min was brought to the United States at the age of one from South Korea. His daily life and future aspirations as a college graduate are stifled in many ways. He explains,

> Being undocumented is like being an invisible person. You have these invisible bars and you are trapped there, sometimes you are by yourself, but most of the time you are there with your whole family. They just do not want to talk about this. From what I understand . . . they feel ashamed they could not give their kids legal status, so what happens is that all these kids become depressed and anxious and worried and feel frustrated that now they can't go to school, they can't get the money to go to school, they can't drive either. I mean these are things you want to do as a young adult. You can't vote, you can't study abroad, you can't go back for vacation to South Korea. The reason why nobody wants to speak about it is because they see the fear of deportation. If I get deported to South Korea that's it; it is over for me.

Minors who must await their cases to be heard are placed in one of three types of facilities. Those with psychological issues are sent to therapeutic programs; minors who have a criminal background or behavioral issues go to secure programs where they are closely monitored; and undocumented minors without serious criminal backgrounds, psychological disorders, or behavioral needs go to one of over forty facilities across the country that allow them greater freedoms while still being held in custody. These facilities often look more like homes than prisons. The detainees held there are usually in their teenage years, but can be much, much younger (there have been five-year-olds smuggled into the country who eventually end up in these facilities). They are provided with home-cooked meals, receive an education, and take part in extracurricular activities such as sports, art, and sometimes field trips. While this may sound like an ideal setup, the detainees are still in a tight security setting, with their movements closely monitored through alarm systems. They must wear uniforms that generally

Figure 4.3. Undocumented youth are increasingly coming out of the shadows to fight for their rights. The New York State Youth Leadership Council held a press conference during their hunger strike in support of the DREAM Act.

IMMIGRANTS GIVING BACK

Most immigrants come to the United States to find jobs that allow them to earn significantly more than they could earn in their home countries. In order to support family members back home, many immigrants send them remittances, a portion of the money they earn in the United States. Family members may come to depend on these funds to meet their everyday needs of food, shelter, and education. Certain countries' economies are so reliant on remittances that this money makes up a large part of the nation's GDP (gross domestic product), the overall value of goods and services produced within a nation. Some people consider remittances an informal type of financial aid from the United States. The following are the 2009 totals sent to the top four countries that received money from immigrants in the United States:[23]

- India—$49 billion
- China—$48 billion
- Mexico—$22 billion
- Philippines—$20 billion

69

consist of sweatpants, sweatshirts, and flip-flops, except when they leave the premises for trips. The minors in these centers must grow up quickly, as they are assigned lawyers who present their cases to immigration judges. They attend court hearings and take part in decisions regarding whether to return home or continue to fight their case in the United States. The majority of these minors are unsuccessful in being allowed to stay in the United States and must return to their home country.

While many teenagers eagerly await their eighteenth birthday, which signals their official entry into adulthood, it is quite the opposite for undocumented detainees. Usually, the day they turn eighteen, undocumented teens must leave the relatively comfortable and safe environment of the juvenile immigration detention center. Uniformed police officers arrive at the center to pick up the eighteen-year-old, handcuff him or her, and transport the young person to an adult detention center. A harsh prison reality becomes the new home.

RELATED RESOURCES

Books

The Secret Story of Sonia Rodriguez, by Alan Lawrence Sitomer (New York: Hyperion, 2008)—This is a fictional story about a U.S.-born fifteen-year-old girl named Sonia, who is the daughter of undocumented Mexican immigrants. The book presents her struggles as she strives to succeed academically while juggling family responsibilities.

Underground America: Narratives of Undocumented Lives (Voices of Witness), by Peter Orner (San Francisco, CA: McSweeny's, 2008)—The book presents the firsthand experiences of twenty-four undocumented men and women from various parts of the world. They speak of the constant fear, obstacles, and dehumanizing working conditions they face each day in the United States.

Just Like Us: The True Story of Four Mexican Girls Coming of Age in America, by Helen Thorpe (New York: Scribner, 2009)—The book follows four inseparable high school friends, all of Mexican descent, living with their families in Denver. However, their friendship is tested after two of the girls learn they are undocumented and confront the daily challenges of being out of status in the United States.

Coyotes: A Journey across Borders with America's Illegal Migrants, by Ted Conover (New York: Vintage Books, 1987)—The author documents the arduous journey of undocumented immigrants as they pay a coyote to take them to the United States.

Enrique's Journey: The Story of a Boy's Dangerous Odyssey to Reunite with His Mother, by Sonia Nazario (New York: Random House, 2006)—This is the story of Enrique, a sixteen-year-old who undertakes a journey as an unaccompanied, undocumented immigrant from Honduras to the United States to be reunited with his mother. As a single mother, she left him when he was five years old to come to the United States to seek out a better future.

Movies

The Visitor (2007)—This is a drama that develops when a college professor and recent widower discovers a couple of undocumented immigrants, a Syrian musician and his Senegalese girlfriend, living in his New York apartment. The professor eventually invites the couple to stay and an unusual friendship blooms.

La Misma Luna (Under the Same Moon) (2007)—This movie depicts the story of a nine-year-old boy who embarks on a journey from Mexico to reunite with his mother, an undocumented worker in the United States.

Papers (2009)—This documentary tells the stories of undocumented youth and their struggles as they come of age without legal status in the United States.

NOTES

1. Nancy Zuckerbrod, "Illegal Students Await Immigration Plan," *USA Today*, June 3, 2007, www.usatoday.com/news/washington/2007–06–03-immigration-students_n.htm (accessed September 30, 2008).

2. Jeffrey S. Passel and D'vera Cohen, "A Portrait of Unauthorized Immigrants in the United States," Pew Hispanic Center, April 14, 2009, pewhispanic.org/files/reports/107.pdf (accessed December 29, 2009).

3. Passel and Cohen, "A Portrait of Unauthorized Immigrants in the United States."

4. David Gonzalez, "A Family Divided by 2 Words, Legal and Illegal," *New York Times*, April 25, 2009, www.nytimes.com/2009/04/26/nyregion/26immig.html?_r=1 (accessed January 21, 2010).

5. Gonzalez, "A Family Divided by 2 Words."

6. Passel and Cohen, "A Portrait of Unauthorized Immigrants in the United States."

7. UNICEF, *State of the World's Children* (New York: UNICEF, 2009), www.unicef.org/sowc09/docs/SOWC09-FullReport-EN.pdf (accessed January 5, 2009).

8. Robert Gonzales, "Young Lives on Hold: The College Dreams of Undocumented Students," College Board, April 2009, professionals.collegeboard.com/profdownload/young-lives-on-hold-college-board.pdf (accessed December 7, 2009).

9. Assistant Secretary for Planning and Evaluation, "The 2009 HHS Poverty Guidelines," U.S. Department of Health and Human Services, updated April 16, 2010, aspe.hhs.gov/poverty/09poverty.shtml (accessed January 21, 2010).

10. Jeanne Brooks-Gunn and Greg J. Duncan, "The Effects of Poverty on Children," *The Future of Children* 7, no. 2 (1997): pp. 55–71.

11. Author, "Distribution of Unauthorized Immigrant Workers Compared to US-Born Workers by Major Occupation Group, 2008," Procon.org, immigration.procon.org/view.resource.php?resourceID=000845#graphs (accessed March 31, 2010).

12. Isabel Martínez, "What's Age Gotta Do with It? Understanding the Age-Identities and School-Going Practices of Mexican Immigrant Youth in New York City," *The High School Journal*, April/May 2009, p. 43.

13. Martínez, "What's Age Gotta Do with It?," p. 43.

14. Martínez, "What's Age Gotta Do with It?," pp. 34–48.

15. Deepa Fernandes, *Targeted: Homeland Security and the Business of Immigration* (New York: Seven Stories Press, 2007), p. 50.

16. Social Justice Class of Pan American International High School, *On the Edge of My New Life* (New York: Social Justice Class of Pan American International High School, 2009), p. 47.

17. Social Justice Class of Pan American International High School, *On the Edge*, p. 28.

18. Social Justice Class of Pan American International High School, *On the Edge*, p. 36.

19. GlobalSecurity.org, "US-Mexico Border Fence / Great Wall of Mexico Secure Fence," www.globalsecurity.org/security/systems/mexico-wall.htm (accessed January 10, 2010).

20. Fernandes, *Targeted*, p. 39.

21. Ann Farmer, "Under Age and Alone, Immigrants See a Softer Side of Detention," *New York Times*, July 14, 2009, www.nytimes.com/2009/07/15/nyregion/15minors.html (accessed February 12, 2010).

22. Lydialyle Gibson, "Nobody's Child," *University of Chicago Magazine* 4 (March/April 2008), p. 36.

23. Dilip Ratha, Sanket Mohapatra, and Ani Silwal, "Migration and Development Brief 12," World Bank, April 23, 2010, econ.worldbank.org/WBSITE/EXTERNAL/EXTDEC/EXTDECPROSPEC TS/0,,contentMDK:21121930~menuPK:3145470~pagePK:6416540 1~piPK:64165026~theSitePK:476883,00.html (accessed October 9, 2009).

5 Refugees and Asylees

"One morning . . . my father went to take prayer water then we heard him go outside. Then when my mother went outside, my father was killed, my sister was outside too. My big sister, but she's dead. She was outside. When they shoot my father, she went to touch my father and they killed my sister. And that morning me and my mother and my brothers that's the time my big brother sent a resettlement to us . . . they hate Muslims over there so they came and killed my father like that. . . . The war is in the place, everybody's running away to go, you don't even look at each other's face. That's the time my big brother got lost from us. He went in Conakry. I don't know how he managed to have papers to come in the United States. We went to Guinea, different part of Guinea. My brother sent papers to us then we come here in United States."

—Mama, Sierra Leone, 17 years old[1]

Migrants who are classified as refugees and asylees, or asylum seekers, make up a small subgroup of immigrants. They come to the United States because they experienced persecution in their home countries. Persecution is defined as consistent mistreatment due to being part of a group or organization that is discredited by another group. According to the 1951 United Nations (UN) Convention, refugees and asylees are individuals or groups who have suffered in their country due to their race, religion, nationality, membership in

"We didn't go to regular school because we couldn't, it was too far and parents wouldn't let their children go that far when the bombing was still there."

—Aida, Bosnia, 17 years old[2]

a specific social group, or political opinion.[3] Because they are not provided protection from their government and because they may be in direct opposition to their government, most of these people cannot return home due to the danger of continued persecution. Refugees are given permission to enter the United States either on an individual basis or as a part of a group that has experienced a similar form of persecution, whereas asylum seekers first enter the country and then request permission to stay. The United States is one of eighteen nations that accept refugees for permanent resettlement, and of those nations, it takes in the highest number of refugees.[4] Nevertheless, only certain individuals and groups are actually permitted to come into the country as refugees or asylees. Over the last twenty-five years, the United States has accepted 1.8 million refugees. Once they have lived in the United States for one year as refugees or asylees, they must apply for lawful permanent resident status. Then after five years they can apply to become naturalized citizens.

A historical review of people granted refugee status in the United States shows that the "where" matters more than the "what." In other words, where the refugees come from has been of greater priority than what kind of persecution they experienced and the difficulties associated with it. Since 1945 three countries—Cuba, Vietnam, and the former Soviet Union—have made up the majority of refugees accepted into the United States based on political persecution. These three nations all have had one thing in common: they all had communist governments. Because of the strong anticommunism position taken by the U.S. government, those seeking refugee status from communist nations have historically received favoritism in the application process. However, individuals from other countries who have been persecuted for reasons other than communism or who lived in countries with good relationships with the United States have generally had a difficult time getting refugee status.

The Refugee Act of 1980 aimed to create a fair playing field so that all individuals and groups applying for refugee status would be considered on an equal basis. The act stated that refugee status was to be considered for all five areas listed in the 1951 UN Convention and required the president and Congress to set the number of refugees the United States would accept on a yearly basis. However, at the same time that the Refugee Act aimed to expand the definition of who could be granted refugee status, it also allowed the United States the possibility of limiting those admitted into the country through decreasing the numerical limits, often referred to as quotas. Figure 5.1 shows the most common countries of origin of refugees in the United States between 1997 and 2007.

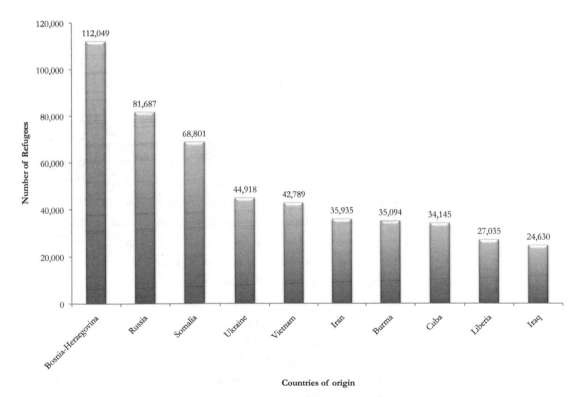

Figure 5.1. Top refugee-sending countries from 1997 to 2007[5]

In 2009 the U.S. government set the limit/quota for total number of refugees at 80,000 for the year. However, there were further limits based on the part of the world the migrants came from. For example, refugees from the Middle East and South Asia were given the highest number of spots (35,000). This region includes individuals from nations such as Iraq, Bhutan, and Iran. The region with the second-highest limit was East Asia (20,500). Refugees from this part of the world came from Burma, Vietnam, and China. The region with the third-highest limit was Africa (15,500). Europe, Latin America, and the Caribbean each had less than 5,000 spots available to them.[6] By looking at the limits allotted to each part of the world, it's clear there is a connection between the political events taking place there and the willingness of the United States to accept a country's refugees.

For many refugees it was never their wish to come to the United States, although they are grateful for the opportunity to live in a place where their rights are protected regardless of their beliefs, affiliations, or background. Most refugees have experienced many hardships before they set foot in the United States. It is not uncommon for them to have experienced traumatic brushes with violence and death, as well as movement into and out of different countries and refugee camps. Once people experience persecution in their nation, they usually escape by heading to a border country, often in masses, and end up residing in refugee camps that form due to the large numbers of migrants who need a place to stay. These temporary communities can be very difficult places to live, with tents for housing, limited rations of food for families, and few educational and job-related opportunities. People can spend a short time there or can end up staying there for years. The average stay is ten years, but can be even longer. For example, in the 1980s Sudanese who fled to Kenya to escape the civil war in their nation spent over twenty years in refugee camps. When living in nearby countries seeking safety and shelter, individuals are interviewed by the United Nations Refugee Agency (UNHCR), the branch of the United Nations responsible for the protection of refugees worldwide. The interviews result in one

Figure 5.2. A young child in a refugee camp in Darfur, Sudan. Photo courtesy of the International Rescue Committee/Gerald Martone/ theirc.org.

of the following decisions for the migrants: (1) to repatriate, or voluntarily return to, the home country, as long as it is safe to do so; (2) to remain in the nearby country where they have sought asylum; or 3) to resettle in a third country such as the United States, Canada, or Australia.[7]

Unlike most other immigrants, who select where they reside in the United States, usually based on the availability of jobs and location of family and friends, refugees are settled by resettlement agencies and usually spread out across the United States. The determination of where they will reside is made by the UNHCR. The goal is to settle refugees in locations where they may have family or in a community where people from their ethnic group already reside, but this is not always possible. The top places to receive refugees in the United States between 1983 and 2004 were New York, New York; Los Angeles, California; Chicago, Illinois; Orange County, California; and Seattle, Washington.[8] The locations are drastically different from their home nations, and often there are few people from the same ethnic group for them to connect with. Therefore, many refugees have a second migration as they move to another place where they can live among people from their own ethnic, racial, religious, and national backgrounds.

When refugees are first settled into a new community in the United States, they receive services that set them apart from any other immigrant group. Organizations such as the International Rescue Committee, Hebrew Immigrant Aid Society, and Church World Service are involved in what is called refugee resettlement. The government provides money through grants to such agencies, and in collaboration with private donations, newly arrived refugees are provided with basic needs such as housing, food, and clothing, as well as social services, including medical, education, and employment assistance as they acclimate to their new surroundings.

ECONOMICS: A PECULIAR ABSENCE

You may have noticed that refugee or asylee status is not granted to anyone who suffers economic hardships. Therefore, the majority of poor people living and suffering from poverty worldwide do not qualify to become refugees or asylees. This group is often referred to as economic migrants when they cross borders in search of better opportunities. They often become undocumented immigrants, as in the case of many Mexicans in the United States.

AN UNCOMMON REFUGEE

Pape Mbaye was a teenager growing up in the West African country of Senegal. However, he was anything but a typical teenager in an Islamic nation that looks down upon homosexuality. He knew early on that he was gay and did not try to hide it, unlike many individuals living in such nations where being gay or lesbian is openly banned. In his early 20s, Pape made a name for himself as a griot, someone who sang and told stories at special events such as weddings and birthdays. In the artist community of Dakar, the nation's capital, he lived among other gay people, where he felt safe and free to develop his sense of self. Then a photograph was printed in the newspaper of what was thought to be a gay wedding ceremony, with a caption stating that Pape Mbaye was an organizer of the event. At that moment everything changed. After being arrested and released a few days later, he was constantly under attack by the police, the media, and mobs, who scrawled antigay graffiti and looted his apartment. Gangs came after Pape and his friends with broken glass, forks, and other weapons and proceeded to beat them. He tried to escape to different parts of Senegal and fled even further into The Gambia, a neighboring country. However, when the Gambian president called for the beheading of gays, he returned to Senegal and found the group Human Rights Watch. Through its assistance, Pape was able to get refugee status and eventually made his way to New York City.[9]

Attaining refugee status for being persecuted as a homosexual has not been very common throughout U.S. immigration history, although it does fall into the social group category of the 1951 UN Convention. There are no known statistics for this small refugee population, but it is becoming more common for gays and lesbians to come to the United States as asylum seekers.

ASYLEES AND ASYLUM SEEKERS

"I was born in El Salvador during the early period of the Salvadorian civil war. . . . At the age of five . . . I witnessed my grandmother's limbs smeared on the pavement. . . . At six, my twenty-year-old mother had fled the country for fear of persecution. At nine, my father had been killed for his involvement in the civil war. At eleven, I held in my hands an M-16 and was told to shoot anything that interferes with the struggle. At twelve, I was kidnapped and held captive for eleven months. In 1993 I traveled by myself across Guatemala and Mexico so that I could be with my mother."

—Marlo, El Salvador, asylee[10]

A SIXTH CATEGORY? ENVIRONMENTAL REFUGEES

Natural or environmental causes do not fall within the five areas outlined in the 1951 UN Convention that defines refugees and asylees. However, there are a growing number of people throughout the world who are being forced to leave their homes due to natural disasters such as fires, floods, tsunamis, and earthquakes. Some people do not cross international borders but must leave their towns and cities. For example, after Cyclone Sidr hit Bangladesh in 2007, huge chunks of land became uninhabitable because the agricultural land was saturated with seawater. The villagers, who have become internally displaced persons, moved to the country's capital, Dhaka, and resettled in the slums there. They do not consider themselves citizens of Dhaka and long to return to their villages; however, they know that they will not be able to live there. With further environmental degradation, Bangladesh will see massive movements of people, many into neighboring India. Once they cross the international border, should they become refugees? It remains to be seen whether environmental issues will be added to the UN categories that allow one to qualify for refugee or asylee status.

WHO IS A REFUGEE?

Katrina was the name given to a hurricane that devastated parts of Louisiana, Mississippi, and Florida in 2005. Many people lost their homes and had to relocate to other parts of the country as a result of this powerful storm. These displaced people were widely referred to as refugees in the media. As a result, widespread outrage erupted due to the way the term *refugee* was being used, as the word had generally been designated for people displaced from their countries, not for citizens within a nation. Many of the people most negatively affected by the storm who were forced to relocate were predominantly African American and lived in poverty. This fact led people to question whether the use of the term *refugee* was intended to mean that they were not viewed as Americans (as opposed to White, middle-class citizens). Do you think the refugee label was used accurately to describe the people who were displaced due to Hurricane Katrina? Why or why not?

Internally displaced persons is a term used to refer to individuals who have had to leave their homes due to circumstances similar to refugees, but do not cross over into another country. This term has not been used in the United States, but has been commonly used in certain parts of the world, especially in developing nations. Do you think it describes the reality of those people affected by Hurricane Katrina better than the term *refugee*?

The difference between asylees and refugees is mostly determined by location. Both groups must show that they have a credible fear of persecution related to the five areas outlined in the 1951 UN Convention. The difference is that refugees seek permission to enter the United States from outside of the country, whereas asylum seekers first come to the United States and then apply for asylum status. While it is possible to receive asylum status at a land border or airport, the chances of it being granted are very low and the possibility of imprisonment is high as people wait for their case to be reviewed. Therefore, many asylum seekers enter the country without permission, as unauthorized immigrants, and then seek legal assistance to begin the asylee application process through the court system.[11] If an asylum seeker's case is denied, the person is ordered to leave the country, often through deportation. The chance of an immigration judge granting an asylum seeker the status of asylee is low. In general 69 percent of cases are denied. The chance of being rejected goes up to 93 percent when a migrant does not have an attorney to assist in the case.[12]

REFUGEE COMMUNITIES IN THE UNITED STATES

Many refugee groups from specific countries are clustered throughout the United States. Each group has its own challenges specific to what they encountered in their home country, as refugees living in neighboring nations, and then in resettlement cities in the United States. Below you will learn about three unique groups of refugees that reside in different parts of the United States.

Soviet Jews in Columbus, Ohio

Jews from the Union of Soviet Socialist Republics (USSR) are a large percentage of the refugee population and can be found in most metropolitan cities across the United States. As a group, they migrated to America in order to escape a communist government and anti-Semitism, prejudice or hatred toward Jews that had been constant in the region dating back to the Middle Ages. Living as Jews in the Soviet Union meant they were not permitted to practice their religion in public, limited in their educational and work-related opportunities, and verbally and physically abused for their religious background. As a result of this anti-Semitism, coupled with the communist government that was in place until the fall of the Soviet Union in 1991, Soviet Jews were able to attain refugee status and relocate to countries such as the United States, Canada, and Israel. A significant group of political refugees (including myself) came to the Midwestern region of Columbus, Ohio, between the mid-1970s and the mid-1990s. The Columbus Jewish Federation (CJF) sponsored the group after it arrived. The refugees were met at the airport by the CJF staff, taken to apartments that had been rented for them, shown around their new town, and provided with English classes in order to support their transition.

The Soviet Jews who arrived in Columbus, Ohio, were often put up in just a few apartment complexes so that they could live close to one another. One complex in Columbus was informally referred to as "Russian Village" after the group took over many of its apartments. The majority of the families were made up of three generations: children, parents, and grandparents. Many of the older generation had fought in World War II or lived through horrific events that accompany wars such as starvation, death of loved ones, and torture. Most of the people from this generation had limited English skills and minimal formal education. For them, learning a new language at an older age was an uphill battle, as was preparing for the naturalization exam that required them to demonstrate spoken and written English abilities (see chapter 10). On the other hand, their children, who were young to middle-aged adults, had a background in English and many came with higher levels of formal education and careers in fields such as engineering, accounting, and science. However, many refugees with advanced college degrees from the USSR found that their degrees meant very little in the United States when it came to finding good jobs. Having higher levels of formal education probably helped in general, but not at first.

People holding doctorates from the Soviet Union had to start out washing dishes in restaurants or mowing lawns. But over time, many were able to establish themselves in their original line of work and were able to move out of the apartments where they were first resettled. Many people in this category bought homes in and around the Columbus area, as well as in other states. Meanwhile, the older generation tended to stay in the apartments provided by the CJF so that they could have a community of people who spoke their language(s), understood their background, and socialized with each other on a regular basis. After settling in to their new place, all the refugees were expected to repay the full price of their airplane tickets.

As a group, Soviet Jewish refugees have acclimated well to the United States. Those who joined the workforce were able to establish themselves in their original careers, purchase homes, and raise their children, some of whom were also refugees and others who were U.S. born. They have benefited from the support provided to them as refugees and have taken advantage of living in a land where economic, social, and religious freedoms are available to them.

Hmong in Madison, Wisconsin

The Hmong people (pronounced "mung") are descendants of an ethnic group from the Southeast Asian nation of Laos. They are Vietnam War–era refugees who were forced to fight for the United States against communism from 1959 to 1975. The United States promised to protect the Hmong, who traditionally lived in the rural hills of Laos. However, the United States never honored its promise. The group was eventually persecuted by the Laotians' newly formed communist government for siding with the United States, in spite of them being forced to do so. Due to their treatment in Laos, Hmong people had to flee their nation by wading across the MeKong River, carrying their children on their backs. They made it to the neighboring countries of China, Vietnam, and Thailand without any possessions.

The Hmong have been coming to the United States as refugees since the mid-1970s. Prior to resettling in the United States, many Hmong spent time in refugee camps in Thailand, where conditions were difficult. The Hmong had to live with limited availability of water, toilets, food, jobs, land to grow food, and education. Most Hmong living in the Thai refugee camps were given permission by the UNHCR to resettle in the United States as refugees. But many held out in hopes of either returning to Laos or remaining in Thailand. However, the Thai government made it clear that it no longer welcomed their presence. After years of residence in deplorable camps, Hmong refugees made their way to the United States.

By the year 2000 there were 186,000 Hmong living in the United States, with the largest concentrations in California, Minnesota, and Wisconsin. Wisconsin, a state with an overwhelming majority White population, at nearly 90 percent, and an Asian population of only 2 percent, may not seem like an ideal destination for the Hmong group.[13] Nevertheless, they have made a place for themselves in the state that offered a strong industrial economy where jobs were more easily available for those without formal education. They developed a Hmong radio station, broadcasting in their native language about Hmong culture and news in Wisconsin and elsewhere. The Hmong are also active in community-based organizations in the area. After their arrival, the public schools began to offer bilingual education programs where students learn through Hmong and English.

The first wave of Hmong was supported by resettlement agencies such as Catholic Charities and United Refugee Services, while later groups were also cosponsored by family members already living in the United States. The early wave of Hmong refugees was provided with thirty-six months of financial assistance, thanks to the Refugee Cash Assistance program, whereas those who came since the early 2000s only had eight months to become financially independent and find work. Most Hmong come with little formal education. They have experience working as farmers, soldiers, and artisans. However, over time they have increased their educational attainment and have found work in many sectors of the economy. The majority have found work in manufacturing, sales, and service positions, although they are also entering professional fields such as medicine, education, and law.

Most Hmong learn English through ESL (English as a Second Language) classes provided to them in Wisconsin. In addition many take Hmong literacy (a language that was primarily oral until the 1950s) in community-based language programs as a way to maintain their native language. Beyond language learning, the Hmong have many other needs when they first arrive. They need to become familiar with "housing, getting the kids enrolled in school, teaching them how to ride the bus, how to get around and survive in this country—how to find the grocery store, use appliances, use the phone."[14]

Children who grew up in refugee camps in Thailand attended Thai schools, but they were only allowed to do so until the age of twelve. Therefore, those who arrived in the United States as teenagers had a hard time in school because of the years they had missed, not to mention the challenges with learning the English language. It is perhaps due to their limited educational background that Hmong youth are at high risk of dropping out of high school. Others leave school early to help support their family financially, as one child is selected to go to complete high school and go on to college while the others go to work. Among those that complete high school, only 3 percent graduate from college.[15] However, these statistics may very well change as a second generation of Hmong in Wisconsin and elsewhere in the United States take advantage of the educational opportunities provided to them.

Somalis in Lewiston, Maine

The Somali Bantus are a minority ethnic group who come from their native Somalia, a nation in the east of Africa. As a group they face persecution in their country from the Cushitic majority, who view the Bantus as second-class citizens. Since Somalia has been in the midst of a civil war since 1992, the Somali Bantus have suffered greatly through violence and the forced loss of their land. After the war began, many relocated to neighboring Kenya and spent years in overcrowded and under-resourced refugee camps, before nearly twelve thousand refugees were given permission to resettle throughout the United States.[16] Those selected to make the journey to the United States bring with them the skills they developed as farmers, but most "have never turned on an electric light switch, used a flush toilet, crossed a busy street, ridden in a car or an elevator, seen snow or experienced air conditioning."[17] Therefore, life in any city or town in the United States leads to new experiences on a variety of levels.

One community to receive Somali refugees was the small town of Lewiston, Maine. It used to be a community that faced low job rates, high crime rates, and an exodus of its young people, leaving behind an aging population. In 2001 the future for the town was bleak until an unexpected and initially unwelcome turn of events occurred: the arrival of East African refugees. It started when a family of Somali refugees settled in Lewiston, which was a mostly European American community in a state with a 95 percent White population. The Somalis felt it was a relatively inexpensive place to live and raise their families, so they let other Somali refugees know about Lewiston, and eventually word spread to other African groups such as the Congolese and Sudanese. By 2009 there were four thousand refugees who called Lewiston home. At first the residents did not welcome these foreign refugees with open arms. Their differences were many; the newly arrived refugees spoke little to no English, had a distinct culture, and practiced the Muslim religion. The mayor even wrote a letter begging the Somalis to stop bringing their friends and family to the town. The original community members were fearful of the impact the Somali Bantus would have on the already poor economy, and they wondered what would happen to their jobs and who was going to pay for the social services the refugees would need, including education and health care. However, over time the African refugees took an active role in the Lewiston economy, opening stores with names such as Mogadishu and

Baracka, importing goods from Africa, and selling traditional clothes, halal foods, and phone cards to the region. As the years passed the economy began to turn around, schools that were in danger of closing became populated again, and the community embraced the infusion of diversity from the new immigrant population. Just as Lewiston helped the Somalis and other refugees rebuild their lives, the refugees similarly brought a dying town back to life.[18]

DIFFERENTIAL TREATMENT: THE CASE OF CUBAN AND HAITIAN MIGRANTS

Cubans have a long history of fleeing to the United States and being accepted here, regardless of their status. The U.S. government has always stood against the communist ways of former president Fidel Castro (and his brother, Raúl Castro). As a way to oppose the Cuban communist revolution, the United States welcomed and even financially supported Cubans escaping their home country. The early waves of Cubans were largely White, highly educated professionals such as doctors, scientists, and academics. Over time

JUNE 20: WORLD REFUGEE DAY

In 2000 the UN General Assembly passed Resolution 55/76, which recognizes June 20 as World Refugee Day. Following in the tradition of many African nations with extremely high concentrations of persecuted people, which had celebrated this subgroup of migrants on different days and weeks, the UN adopted the resolution to expand recognition of this day and to stand in solidarity with Africa, a continent with extremely high levels of persecuted individuals. UNHCR goodwill ambassador and actress Angelina Jolie has used her celebrity status to bring attention to the cause of refugees around the globe on this day and beyond.

the immigrants became increasingly non-White and less educated, and the United States was less enthusiastic about their arrival.[19] In 1966 the Cuban Adjustment Act passed to automatically provide Cubans who make it onto U.S. soil with asylum status. This policy, referred to as "wet foot, dry foot," specifies that any Cuban caught at sea with "wet feet" has to be sent back, whereas those who make it onto U.S. soil with "dry feet" are automatically granted asylum without the need to prove persecution in Cuba. This policy gives Cubans immigration rights that set them apart from anyone else seeking asylum in the United States, especially their neighbors to the east, in Haiti.

The U.S. history with Haiti, the poorest nation in the Western Hemisphere, has been complicated and difficult. The nation has experienced a great deal of political turmoil, including government coups and dictatorships, which has pushed many Haitians to seek a better life in the United States. Since flying was mostly just an option for those with government permission to leave the country, many Haitians took to the sea by boat to escape their harsh realities. However, the sea provided many obstacles, specifically those put in place by the U.S. government. The Coast Guard specifically looked to stop Haitians in their tracks. President George H. W. Bush instructed that the Haitian migrants either be returned without being questioned about any persecution they may have experienced or be sent to a prison in Guantánamo Bay, Cuba, which has recently become notorious for holding individuals accused of playing a role in terrorism in the United States. Since 1995 more than thirty-four thousand Haitians were held there and just over 10,000 were allowed to come to the United States. The rest were eventually returned to Haiti. The early 1990s was also a time when the U.S. Coast Guard surrounded Haiti with over twenty ships and patrol boats as well as airplanes to guard the seas and ensure that Haitians would not set off toward the United States. This barricade was referred to as a "floating Berlin Wall, around those seeking freedom."[20] In 2005 Haitians who made it onto U.S. soil had a 17 percent chance of actually getting asylum, or an 83 percent chance of being denied.[21]

Due to the tragic 2010 earthquake in Haiti, the United States changed its policies for Haitians already in the United States. All those awaiting deportation to Haiti would not be sent back and out-of-status Haitians would be granted temporary asylum status, allowing them to stay and work in the country for eighteen months. It was presumed that they would also "send remittances back to Haiti as the nation 'gets back on its feet.'"[22] However, the U.S. government also made it clear that any Haitians trying to make it to the United States to escape the devastation of the earthquake without authorization would be sent back.

Although the United States relaxed its strict approach to Haitian migrants and asylum seekers, there has been a drastic difference between the U.S. policies directed at Cubans and those for Haitians. The disparity in treatment does not lie in the persecution and difficulties experienced in their home countries, but in the type of governments they come from and their relationship with the United States. Additionally, the issues of race and socioeconomic class—poor and Black Haitians as opposed to the more diverse Cubans, who include educated Whites—likely play into the decisions made regarding the asylum of individuals from these two nations. Although ninety miles separate Cuba and Haiti, they are worlds apart when it comes to U.S. immigration policy.

RELATED RESOURCES

Books

A Long Way Gone: Memoirs of a Boy Soldier, by Ishmael Beah (New York: Farrar, Straus and Giroux, 2007)—This memoir vividly recounts the author's experiences growing up in the African nation of Sierra Leone during the country's civil war of the 1990s. The book takes the reader through the young boy's violence-filled years as a child soldier and his path to the United States as a refugee.

Outcasts United: A Refugee Team, an American Town, by Warren St. John (New York: Spiegel & Grau, 2009)—The reader meets three soccer teams (the Fugees) made up of refugee boys from war-torn African, Middle Eastern, and Balkan nations. The boys are resettled in the southern state of Georgia, where they play against mostly White, middle-upper-class teams. Their story goes beyond sport, to broader global and local politics.

Movies

Sierra Leone's Refugee All Stars: A Documentary Film (2005)—This documentary follows six refugees from civil war–ravaged Sierra Leone as they reside in a refugee camp in the Republic of Guinea. They create a band, called the Refugee All Stars, that uses music as a way in which to deal with the horrors they have experienced. They are also able to share their stories through their music, which has brought them international recognition.

Sentenced Home (2006)—This documentary is about three Cambodian American men who must return to their country after stricter immigration laws were passed following 9/11. The men were brought to the United States as children by their refugee families.

Website

The New Wave (2009), www.mediathatmattersfest.org/watch/9/the_next_wave—This documentary shows how the Carteret Islanders are struggling to relocate as the first climate-change refugees.

NOTES

1. Global Action Project, "The Documentary Project for Refugee Youth: Mama," www.global-action.org/refugee/testimonies/mama.html (accessed June 23, 2010).

2. Global Action Project, "The Documentary Project for Refugee Youth: Aida," www.global-action.org/refugee/testimonies/aida.html (accessed June 23, 2010).

3. The UN Refugee Agency, "Convention and Protocol Relating to the Status of Refugees," last updated September 7, 2007, p. 5, www.unhcr.org/3b66c2aa10.html (accessed April 23, 2010).

4. There are many more countries, especially those that border the home country of persecuted individuals, where refugees reside. However, these refugee camps are usually meant to be temporary residences, although many refugees may stay at these sites for years.

5. Kelly J. Jefferys and Daniel C. Martin, "Refugees and Asylees: 2007," U.S. Department of Homeland Security, July 2008, http://www.dhs.gov/xlibrary/assets/statistics/publications/ois_rfa_fr_2007.pdf (accessed May 2, 2010).

6. Cultural Orientation Resource Center, "US Refugee Program, Current Fiscal Year Admission Statistics," last updated May 2010, www.cal.org/co/refugee/statistics/index.html (accessed May 5, 2010).

7. Cultural Orientation Resource Center, "US Refugee Program."

8. Audrey Singer and Jill H. Wilson, "Refugee Resettlement in Metropolitan America," *Migration Information Source*, March 2007, www.migrationinformation.org/Feature/display.cfm?ID=585 (accessed February 15, 2010).

9. Kirk Semple and Lydia Polgreen, "Persecuted in Africa, Finding Refuge in New York," *New York Times*, October 5, 2008, www.nytimes.com/2008/10/06/nyregion/06pape.html?_r=1&scp=1&sq=asylum%20gay%20africa&st=cse (accessed January 14, 2010).

10. Mario Escobar, "Fighting Another War," in *Underground Undergrads: UCLA Undocumented Immigrants Speak Out*, ed. Gabriela Madera et al. (Los Angeles: UCLA Center for Labor Research and Education, 2008), p. 25.

11. David W. Haines, "Refugees," in *The New Americans: A Guide to Immigration since 1965*, ed. Mary C. Waters and Reed Ueda (Cambridge, MA: Harvard University Press, 2007), pp. 56–69.

12. TRAC Immigration, "Immigration Judges," trac.syr.edu/immigration/reports/160/ (accessed February 5, 2010).

13. U.S. Census Bureau, "State and County QuickFacts: Wisconsin," quickfacts.census.gov/qfd/states/55000.html (accessed December 1, 2009).

14. Brenda Ingersoll, "For Hmong, a New Home," *Wisconsin State Journal*, May 18, 2004, www.madison.com/wisconsinstatejournal/local/74542.php (accessed November 2, 2009).

15. John Duffy, Roger Harmon, Donald A. Ranard, Bo Thao, and Kou Yang, "The Hmong: An Introduction to Their History and Culture," Culture Profile No. 18, June 2004, www.cal.org/co/hmong/hmong_FIN.pdf (accessed February 4, 2010).

16. The UN Refugee Agency, "Somali Bantus Prepare for Life in America," August 1, 2002, www.unhcr.org/3d493a2f5.html (accessed March 1, 2010).

17. Ray Wilkinson, "A Lucky Few," *Refugees Magazine*, no. 128 (2002), p. 2.

18. Jesse Ellison, "The Refugees Who Saved Lewiston: A Dying Maine Mill Town Gets a Fresh Burst of Energy," *Newsweek*, January 17, 2009, www.newsweek.com/id/180035 (accessed January 15, 2010).

19. Jane Guskin and David L. Wilson, *The Politics of Immigration: Questions and Answers* (New York: Monthly Review Press, 2007), pp. 34–37.

20. Douglas Farah, "Coast Guard Patrols, Clinton's Switch on Repatriation Delay Haitian Exodus," *Washington Post*, January 21, 1993, p. A14.

21. Guskin and Wilson, *The Politics of Immigration*, pp. 34–37.

22. CNN, "Haitians in the US Can Apply for Protected Status," January 15, 2010, www.cnn.com/2010/POLITICS/01/15/haitians.us/index.html?hpt=T2 (accessed January 16, 2010).

6 Homesickness and Cultural Differences

"We feel so sad, we miss our family, and I miss my country because I spent my whole childhood there and my memories are there. I was crying when we left and I am still crying now. Every immigrant has the same story, just the push and pull factors are different."

—Sobia, Pakistan, 18 years old

Change is often difficult. Most individuals experience change when starting a new grade level, going to a different school, or moving to a new city or state. Moving to a new country is a change far fewer people go through, yet it is a life-changing event for an immigrant. The migration process can be exhilarating, horrifying, and every emotion in between at different moments. While there may be new and exciting events that arise in a different country, over time many immigrants may feel a sense of homesickness. Immigrants may miss family members left behind, feel lonely, and feel like an outsider. This chapter will look at the specific ways immigrant youth experience homesickness and how they deal with the differences between the cultures of their home country and the United States.

Homesickness is a natural response to change in one's life. It can surface when moving, going away to college, or going on a long trip. Many teens who come to a new country find they miss their family, friends, school, the ability to easily communicate with people, and a sense of predictability in the routines that were a regular part of their lives. They may also feel left out of the local culture and lost in the sea of movies,

"The more difficult things [about living in the United States] were the fast pace, learning how to take the train, learning a new language, and adapting to new school standards."

—Bryon, Ecuador, 16 years old

pop stars, and social standards that are unfamiliar to them. Even different food or different weather may make a new immigrant feel homesick. This shift from a sense of safety and familiarity to the unknown of a new land affects people in different ways.

Immigration often results in the separation of families. Sometimes this may mean that one's grandparents, aunts, uncles, and cousins will no longer live in the same country. Others may find themselves leaving their siblings or one or both parents in order to immigrate to a new country. This change in family structure creates a difficult situation for an adolescent who no longer has the same support system in place.

"I came to the U.S. because my father was living in Florida for a very long time, and he asked my mom to have me come over because it would mean more opportunities and a better future for me here. So my mom stayed. She is still there and that is kind of bad, but in the future she may come here."
—Maite, Haiti, 16 years old

While for some people, immigration involves leaving family behind, it is just the opposite for others. Reuniting or even meeting family members for the first time also occurs when relatives move to a new country in stages. Often one parent will come and get established by finding housing, getting a job, and earning enough money before sending for everyone else to join him or her. The reunification process can be a very positive experience, but family members who have been apart for long periods of time may feel more like strangers than next of kin. Therefore, it's important to take the time to get to know each other again and reestablish family roles.

"It was the first time to meet my nineteen-year-old brother and twenty-one-year-old sister. They were here since a very long time. I had talked to them by phone, but we never were together. Now we know each other."
—Flore, Haiti, 16 years old

Homesickness is a normal and natural part of the immigration process. How one chooses to deal with homesickness matters. While some people may choose to ignore their feelings, this may result in depression, isolation, or withdrawing from aspects of their new life.

Depression may manifest itself in different ways. Some adolescents may become irritable and begin acting out in school, getting in trouble, or turning to drinking or drugs to deal with their feelings. Sometimes, adolescents struggle with their grades and begin missing or not completing their assignments. Others may feel tired and sleepy, or isolated from family and friends. Some people try to cope with those feelings by eating too little or too much, sleeping too little or too much, skipping school, or not engaging in activities that they used to enjoy. Still other adolescents may deal with the pain by weeping, and others may turn to self-injury (cutting or burning themselves) to deal with their depression. Some may even become suicidal, especially if they struggle with fitting in at their new school or neighborhood. It is important that someone who may be experiencing these feelings seeks appropriate help.

Young people in this situation should reach out to others by discussing their feelings with family members; turning to creative outlets such as writing, composing music, or painting;

万水千山过西洋.
一心渴望再自由,
谁知枸留末匪中.
失望,伤心无人知,
后悔扬帆过西洋,
自由雄鹰哪里寻?
自由地方在哪方?
还为那金山梦 ?

Miao Yu Li

Long, Long journey crossed pacific
poor bird thirst for free land.
Miscarry fall into cage. damn.
Darkness . . .
Sadness . . .
Regret to leave the steady nest.
Regret to hoist the sails.
what a free eagle, Then.
what an opportunity land.
what America dream.
. . . give me a hand.

—Miao Yu Li

Figure 6.1. A poem written in English and Chinese by Miao Yu Li, eighteen years old, a recent immigrant from China

or becoming involved in sports or other activities. In the case of potential suicide, self-injury, or severe depression and hopelessness, it is crucial to find professional help. A school guidance counselor may be a good start, while social service organizations may direct a new immigrant to low-cost agencies where therapy may be available.

On the other hand, adolescents who are open about their feelings, have people to talk to, and look for solutions to their homesickness tend to do better over time. Some people find comfort in talking through their emotions with family members, friends who have gone through similar experiences, or adults in their school such as guidance counselors and teachers. Finding ways to keep in touch with loved ones in the home country is another way to ease the pain of separation. Now there are a variety of options that allow the lines of communication to stay open, in spite of distance. Beyond the telephone and sending letters, there is e-mail, instant messaging, and online voice or video conversations through programs such as Skype. Depending on the availability of technology and the affordability of it, there are now a variety of ways to stay connected with family and friends. A creative way of keeping in touch with relatives or friends who may not have access to the latest technology or may not have the skills to use it (for instance, elderly grandparents) may be putting together care packages of photographs of the family members in the new country, so that the family members in the home country can feel included in the immigration process. These ideas may help in dealing with and eventually lessening the feelings of homesickness.

Another way to maintain a connection to the native country and culture is through joining a group or organization from one's national, religious, or ethnic group. For example, schools may have clubs such as an Asian American Club or Chicano Club. Religious organizations also have groups for youth to connect with others from similar backgrounds. There may be nonprofit organizations, such as the International Rescue Committee, that also address the needs of specific groups to help with acclimation as they allow immigrants to maintain connections with their home culture.

Cultural Differences

The typical ways of behaving, or norms, for young adults in the United States often differ from those of other countries and cultures. Sometimes the differences may just be interesting, but often they differ in ways that directly contradict or conflict with one another. This creates a difficult situation in which adolescents must find ways to negotiate between different cultures as they figure out where their beliefs and values fall. In this chapter you will find a discussion of the cultural issues that teens must navigate after coming into contact with U.S. cultural norms. Of course, the United States is large and very diverse, so some of the areas discussed may differ based on the region of the United States one moves to, as well as the local cultures present.

Clothing/Fashion/Materialism

"In my country girls can't wear pants to school. We wear uniforms and have our hair cut like boys. In my Catholic school they did not want us to waste time. It was their philosophy that if we leave girls with long hair they are going to waste time every morning or night instead of studying. When I moved to the U.S. I learned that your dress code really matters. It took a while for me to know the brand names and little by little I caught up. And then I started making friends."

—Eva, Tanzania, 22 years old

Something that immediately becomes clear to newly arrived immigrant adolescents is how fashion, or the types of clothing, hairstyles, and accessories people wear, often matter in schools and in the lives of teens and young adults. The degree to which fashion matters depends on where one lives (for example, urban cities tend to focus more on style and dress than rural areas), and the peer group one associates with. Depending on the country you come from, the difference in fashion may range from minimal to extreme.

While in their home country, some immigrants never put much thought into the types of clothes they wore or their hairstyles. Those coming from poverty had few options when it came to their daily attire and may have just had one or two shirts, pants, dresses, and/or pair(s) of shoes. However, in the United States, having a variety of clothing options is the norm, but simply having a lot of clothes is not enough. In some places, many teens feel that the clothes must be fashionable, meaning either designer labels or a popular style. Some students who do not adapt their fashion to the mainstream often find themselves being teased or looked down upon by peers. However, there are teens who make it a point to develop their own sense of style that often goes against the majority.

The issue of fashion becomes more complicated when people emigrate from more conservative cultures or religions, as U.S. style tends to be less restrictive. For example, young women who are Muslim or Orthodox Jewish and dress according to the guidelines of their faith may experience a different type of challenge. Because they must dress more conservatively and modestly by covering most of their bodies, their style stands out from the mainstream in the United States. People may wonder why they dress in this particular way. It is possible to still make fashionable choices, even in modest dress, and some people choose to do that. For example, this might mean wearing a floor-length denim skirt as opposed to a miniskirt, or a sweater in a popular style but with longer sleeves. This might allow a young woman to adhere to her religious beliefs but still feel like she is fitting in with her peers.

Most teens and young adults have to make decisions about whether they will continue to dress in the style of clothing from their home country, take on the new styles of their peers, or create a style of their own. However, some schools in the United States require students to wear uniforms. This alleviates the issue of fitting in, at least when it comes to style of dress. Other schools have dress codes that dictate the types of clothing that are permitted. Nevertheless, fashion is something most teen immigrants learn about early on in the United States.

The culture of the United States has been described as "materialistic," meaning that the objects one attains play a large role in determining a person's status. In some cases, people who own lavish homes, fancy cars, expensive electronics, and the most fashionable clothes are often admired and seen as "better than" others who cannot afford or choose not to have such items. This focus on material goods takes away from the focus of who a person is and places the emphasis on what they have. Luis, a recent immigrant, explains the differences between his country and the United States when it comes to materialism: "In the DR [Dominican Republic] people are happy with what they have. They're not like here. If they have something, they want to have more and more until they have everything."

Schools

"There are many differences. Mexican education is more advanced, but the U.S. has more opportunities. In Mexico everyone in school wants to be there. They can kick out people, but in the U.S. you get suspended. In Mexico if you're pregnant and have a baby, you don't have the opportunity to go to school. You have to stay home."

—Angela, Mexico, 17 years old

"I think here the schools are better because you get many classes. There are many opportunities here and many are for free. I was in a private school [in Haiti] and my dad paid $1,500 for my school— it is like being in college, you need to learn and it is your obligation because you are paying and you are responsible for learning. If you don't learn, too bad. You are paying and they will not return your money."

—Katiana, Haiti, 16 years old

"In my country the school systems were strict. Everyone had uniforms, everything goes in order. Everyone follows rules. It's very strict. In this school students have real big freedom. They can say their opinions, they can feel free in this school, they can wear whatever they want. Teachers aren't very strict; they are very friendly to students and that makes me very happy."

—Ramil, Uzbekistan, 16 years old

Most new immigrants eighteen years and under get their first real sense of American culture in schools. But there are many types of schools in the United States, and they differ from each other in significant ways. One difference is that some schools are public, while others are private. Most immigrant students, especially those who are newly arrived to the country, attend public schools, which are free to those who attend. The government pays for public education primarily through tax dollars, because in the United States anyone eighteen or under is entitled to a free public education from kindergarten through twelfth grade. (Many immigrants come from countries where public schools require students, or their families, to pay for education-related expenses such as tuition, books, and extracurricular activities, but this is not the case in public schools in the United States.)

Public schools differ in size, from small to medium to very large, and in their locations, including urban, suburban, and rural settings, and they tend to be segregated according to the socioeconomic class, race, and ethnicity of their communities. Therefore, while the country as a whole is extremely diverse, schools often do not show the true diversity that exists in the nation due to the segregated nature of the neighborhoods in which they are located.

There are many different types of private schools as well. Some have a religious focus (and these tend to be less expensive than other private schools), while others are boarding schools where students live away from their families for extended periods of time. Some private schools may focus primarily on college preparation. Private schools require families to pay for their children's education, and some are so expensive they are only available to those from the upper class who can afford the tuition. (Some private schools offer scholarships that may be available to low-income families.)

Most immigrants attend schools along with their U.S.-born peers. Aside from ESL (English as a Second Language) or bilingual education classes, immigrants generally do not take part in special programs to help them get situated in a new country, culture, and school setting. However, in 2010 there were twenty-eight states with more than sixty schools or specific programs designed just for middle and high school newcomers.[1] These special sites take in newly arrived immigrant students for anywhere from a few months in the summer to one to two school years. In these schools, a student population of newcomers from all over the world (or sometimes from just one specific region) is given special support in developing their English, learning across the subject areas, and adjusting to the new culture of the United States. After a short time in such schools or programs, the students move into general schools where they are mixed in with their U.S.-born and immigrant peers.

There is another type of high school that is specifically designed for immigrant students who have been in the United States for four years or less and still have yet to reach a specific level of English by the time they reach the ninth grade. These schools are part of the Internationals Network for Public Schools, and there were thirteen such high schools in California and New York in 2010.[2] The difference between these schools and newcomer programs is that students complete their entire high school careers in one place and are always and only with other immigrant students (except for special occasions). Most international high schools have students from all over the world, with a mix of Black (mostly Africans and Haitians), Latino, Asian, and White (mostly from Europe) immigrants, while a few of the schools are specifically for native Spanish speakers due to the high Latino population. Therefore, students are able to receive their education bilingually, through English and Spanish. Teens from one such high school in New York City—in which students come from nations such as Haiti, Pakistan, Tajikistan, Mexico, and China—discuss the pros and cons of attending a high school specifically for immigrants:

> *Ying:* I feel sometimes I want to go to another school that has people who were born here; that could help me much better. In this school they are all the same as me—we all are immigrants—so some students help each other, some don't. The children who were born here, they may know more stuff than the child who just came here.
>
> *Sasha:* But this school helps you learn about other cultures and languages, because it's good to learn about other countries.

103

Miguel: Right, they might even know more than an American teenager does. We're in a school where everybody speaks a different language, so other students could help you learn about the culture. They're not gonna make fun of our accents, but if it was another school that only had American children they could say, "I don't like that."

Gender Roles

"In the United States there are sports for men and women. There are more opportunities to get ahead. In Mexico there are no sports teams in some schools because they can't afford it. Also, [in Mexico] sports are supposed to be just for men."
—Sandra, Mexico, 16 years old

Every society has norms, or expectations, for the way boys and girls (and men and women) are supposed to behave. In the United States, as in most other societies, these norms are taught (sometimes in subtle ways) from the first day of a baby's life. When a girl is born she is often dressed in pink and told how pretty she is, whereas a boy is dressed in blue and told that he is smart and strong. This type of socialization into gender roles continues through childhood and into adulthood by the types of toys, activities, and coursework boys and girls are provided within the home, school, and community.

"I am living with my dad and he doesn't want me to study. He doesn't support me because he feels women are supposed to be at home and having children. I want to study law, but my dad says women and politics don't mix. I want to take part in many programs in school, but he doesn't like me to. But I am going to continue because my teachers support me and they say I will have a bright future."
—Maria, Mexico, 15 years old

It is generally the case that societal norms regarding gender are reinforced in schools and other institutions. For example,

MASCULINITIES AND FEMININITIES

While gender roles in the United States have been undergoing a redefinition for many years, some traditional gender norms still persist. Table 6.1 shows some traditional expectations for males and females in the United States that are still held by some people. See how they compare with the norms of other nations and cultures. Also, think about the ways in which you either fit within these norms or differ from them.

girls may be steered toward language arts courses and related careers while boys may be encouraged to take advanced courses in math and science. When it comes to immigrant students, schools may make incorrect assumptions about the gender roles in students' home cultures. For example, in one high school with a large number of Pakistani immigrants, the teachers, guidance counselors, and principal were under the impression that following graduation the girls would be "married off" and not permitted to study at a four-year college. However, the

Table 6.1. Traditional Gender Roles

Male Social Norms	Female Social Norms
Intelligent	Emotional
Good at math and science	Expressive
Aggressive	Verbal
Assertive	Good at language arts
Physically strong	Reliant on men
Does not show emotions or cry	Submissive
Good at or interested in sports (e.g., football, baseball, basketball, or hockey)	Valued based on attractiveness
Valued by earning money	

advice these students were given in school drastically differed from the aspirations of the girls themselves and those of their families. One study found that out of twenty-seven high school Pakistani girls, not even one student expected to be married in the near future and many considered college as an option. This mismatch of perspectives between school officials and immigrant students shows a lack of understanding of how gender roles evolve within cultures over time.[3]

Sexuality

Sexuality is still a taboo topic for some people in the United States, particularly for those who conform to traditional expectations. People who identify as lesbian, gay, bisexual, transgendered, or queer (LGBTQ) may be discriminated against in a variety of ways. For this reason, some people choose to stay "in the closet" or keep their sexuality hidden from their family and friends. However, this has been changing in certain parts of the United States, and teens, even those as young as middle school, have started to speak freely about their sexual identity and live openly as LGBTQ individuals. Some schools have developed clubs, often referred to as Gay-Straight Alliances (GSA), where LGBTQ youth and their straight allies come together to discuss relevant issues and stand up for equal rights.

Some immigrants come from nations where gay issues are discussed openly and are less controversial. However, many immigrants come from countries, cultures, or religions that openly hate, abuse, imprison, or even kill LGBTQ people. Therefore, for some people, coming to the United States where sexuality is discussed and sometimes accepted can be rather shocking.

Dating

Some cultures have very strict norms about teen dating, if it is even permitted at all. For some, the existence of arranged marriages erases the need to date completely. For others, dating is

IMMIGRATION AND DEPRESSION

By Dina Goldstein Silverman, PhD

The changes one experiences starting a life in a new country can be so overwhelming that some immigrants develop depressive symptoms as a result. Below is an example of Aisha, a fourteen-year-old Pakistani immigrant who has recently relocated to a major southwestern city.

Aisha grew up in a tight-knit working-class Pakistani family, where she is the fourth of six children. Her family immigrated to the United States because her father had limited job opportunities in Pakistan. Although Aisha was excited about the new opportunities, including a better job for her father, she was also sad about leaving behind her friends and her older sisters who were married and would remain in Pakistan. In Pakistan, Aisha, a devout Muslim, attended an all-girls school, where she was an A student who wrote poetry and enjoyed playing with her younger cousins, nieces, and nephews. She also took English lessons and was confident about her ability to communicate in English. However, in the United States, Aisha has had to attend public school with both girls and boys and has discovered that she struggles to understand the regional dialect in her school. She feels shy and uncomfortable with boys her age and is torn about whether she wants to date or adhere to her family's traditional values that forbid dating. She also dresses much more modestly than many of her American classmates, including covering her hair with a hijab, wearing long sleeves, and avoiding makeup. There are no other Pakistanis in her school, and while Aisha knows several Indian girls, they have not been friendly toward her, as they are Hindu and come from wealthier families than Aisha's. At home, Aisha shares a room with her two younger sisters and is expected to help them with homework. She is also expected to help with the housework and to translate for her mother, who speaks limited English.

For the past nine months that Aisha has been in the United States, her mood has plummeted, and she feels worried, sad, and irritable more often than not. She frequently cries and finds that she no longer enjoys spending time with her younger sisters, and that she struggles with her homework and has little interest in the things that she used to enjoy, such as writing poetry. Aisha struggles with concentration and has been forgetful lately, while previously, she was attentive and organized. Aisha's mother is worried about Aisha, as she has lost weight and constantly complains of feeling tired. Aisha also feels guilty about leaving her older sisters, nieces, and nephews behind in Pakistan, and finds herself wondering if she might be better off dead, as she feels like she is a burden to her family.

The symptoms that Aisha is experiencing are signs of depression. It would be important for Aisha to speak to a trusted adult at home, at her mosque, or at school about her feelings, especially her recent sense of hopelessness and her thoughts about death. A school guidance counselor would be able to assess Aisha's depression and provide her with referrals for professional help. That could involve meeting with a counselor or psychologist individually or in a group of other teens that are struggling with acculturation and depression, seeing a doctor for medication, and becoming involved in school or community activities.

something that begins when one reaches adulthood. In the United States, dating is often the norm in high school, especially the later years. Schools even have junior and senior (eleventh and twelfth grade) proms, which are often elaborate dances to which students bring dates. Sometimes dating and relationships in high school are evident when couples display their affection for each other in school. For those who come from more traditional cultures that strictly reject dating, this type of environment can be quite jarring. Some teens will choose to follow their home cultural norms and wait to begin dating, whereas others may feel ready to start dating or feel pressured into entering the dating world.

Increased Diversity

"Actually I haven't seen Black people around in Georgia, maybe a few, and when you're seeing them, you're just following them. I thought they are all violent. Plus the Jewish people. I never knew Jewish [people], but there was a Jewish cemetery next to my house. And now I have a lot of Jewish friends."

—Andrei, Georgia, 16 years old

Due to the rich immigration history of the United States, diversity is a cornerstone of the nation. Diversity is present in people's racial, ethnic, linguistic, cultural, and religious backgrounds, just to name a few human and social differences. Many immigrants come from countries that are more homogeneous, meaning people tend to be rather similar to one another in those ways. For some, their move to the United States is the first time they see or come into direct contact with people of different backgrounds from their own. Because immigrants may have had limited interactions with people from other groups, they may view some groups according to the ways they are portrayed in the media—for example, that White people are smart; Black people are criminals, athletes, or rappers; Asians are nerdy and subservient; and Latinos speak only Spanish. However, when one meets and interacts with people from different groups, these stereotypes can be broken down, as people then see that individual diversity exists within every group. This means that within one racial group, for example, there are wide ranges of differences that directly go against the narrow ways in which groups may be perceived.

Generational Clashes

It is well known that parents and their adolescent children may see things from different perspectives. However, for immigrant families, things can become even more complicated. When immigrant adolescents become acclimated to U.S. cultural norms, they may start believing and behaving in ways that directly contradict their home culture. This may cause friction within their families, which can lead to disagreements over the choices adolescents make. Because adult immigrants tend to have beliefs and value systems that are closely tied to their home country and

---

REASONABLE EXPECTATIONS?

Do you feel these are reasonable activities for teens to take part in?

- Going out on a date
- Attending a late-night party with school friends
- Having a sleepover at a friend's house
- Helping family members by translating at doctors' appointments
- Filling out important forms
- Taking care of younger siblings after school and on the weekends

These areas may bring about different reactions in immigrant teens and their parents or families. How you feel about each expectation likely relates to the norms and values you hold. Are there any compromises that can be made so that the views and expectations of multiple generations of immigrants can be met? For instance, parents may not feel comfortable with their teenage daughter dating, but they may feel more at ease with her socializing within a group in a public setting, such as a mall or a skating rink.

culture, and children are still forming their views and are influenced by their surroundings and peers, disagreements are bound to occur. While some disagreement may be inevitable, it is important to seek compromise and keep the lines of communication open to address these conflicts as they arise. Members of the extended family who have been in the United States longer may be a useful resource to help adolescents navigate communication with his or her family.

TRAUMA

"I've been here for three years, but for the first two years I didn't learn anything. I got sick, mental. . . . Because when I came to the United States, I missed my [parents], my family and my friends and my Vietnam."

—Vihn, Vietnam, 18 years old[4]

Most immigrants experience homesickness, which includes feelings of sadness, loneliness, and alienation. There are some who have had experiences in their home country, during the migration process, or in the United States that are extremely difficult and stressful. Some may experience trauma, which can lead to long-term mental and even physical suffering. Trauma is more extreme than homesickness because it takes away an individual's ability to take part in routine events and relationships in everyday life. Traumatic events may happen to an immigrant in his or her country of birth, where that individual may have experienced persecution or was forced into being a child soldier. Trauma may also result from traveling from one country to another, especially in the case of undocumented immigrants who suffer through extreme conditions and dangers to make it to the United States. Furthermore, living in a new country without family members or with the stress of being "found out" or caught in an immigration raid may also lead to extreme difficulty functioning. For everyone, these circumstances are stressful;

POST-TRAUMATIC STRESS DISORDER

By Dina Goldstein Silverman, PhD

Many immigrant children and teenagers who come to the United States have lived through traumatic situations, which can range from witnessing family members, neighbors, and loved ones being murdered, executed, raped, or mutilated, to surviving assault, rape, or mutilation; to being a victim of a violent crime or of a natural disaster, such as an earthquake or a hurricane; to surviving a terror act. Below is an example of Najja, a thirteen-year-old immigrant from Uganda who had been abducted and forced to serve as a child soldier before coming to the United States through the aid of a charitable organization.

Najja was born in a Ugandan village, one of five children. When he was eight, the Lord's Resistance Army invaded his village and kidnapped Najja, along with his older sister Masani and his younger brother Akiki. That day, Najja saw his father, mother, and younger siblings bludgeoned and dismembered. Najja and his two surviving siblings were marched into the bush, where Masani and the other female children were raped and forced to become sex slaves for the members of the Army unit. Najja, Akiki, and the rest of the boys were subjected to beatings and religious indoctrination. They were forced at gunpoint to fight one another to the death in order to make them into tough, brutal soldiers, and at one point, Najja, who was bigger and stronger, was forced to slaughter his younger brother to prove his readiness and strength to his unit commander. Najja was then sent out to other villages, where he killed and maimed locals, including women and children. He was also given little food and subjected to drug use to make him more compliant. When Najja was eleven, his unit was captured, and Najja along with other child soldiers, was disarmed. Najja lived in a camp for child soldiers, where he would come in contact with trauma counselors and a charitable organization that would bring him over to the United States, where Najja is now living with an American family.

Although Najja has made significant progress since he left Uganda, he continues to experience recollections of the atrocities he lived through, including disturbing images of murder and rape and thoughts of death. He also has frequent graphic nightmares, and while awake, he has flashbacks of the events he lived through. Sometimes, Najja thinks he hears his brother begging him for mercy or his sister or mother screaming in pain. Najja also startles easily and is afraid to sleep in the dark. He has a hard time falling asleep and wakes up frequently throughout the night from nightmares. At those times, he is afraid to fall back asleep. Najja attends school but frequently spaces out while in class and does not interact with other students there. He seldom speaks when in school and does not make direct eye contact with his peers or his teachers. He avoids speaking about the trauma he lived through and feels estranged from other students, as well as from his foster family. At times, he becomes irritable and angry and has violent outbursts where he might hurt himself or attack other family members. He is hypervigilant and does not like to be touched. Najja does not believe that he will ever live a long life, and he does not expect to have a job, a career, or a family himself.

Najja is experiencing symptoms indicative of post-traumatic stress disorder. It is important for someone like Najja to be receiving professional help from a mental health professional, such as a psychologist or a psychiatrist, to address his symptoms of trauma. He and his foster family may also benefit from family counseling to help them adapt to living together and facilitate Najja's healing. Najja may also benefit from being involved in a therapy group with children who have been through similar experiences.

for some, these same situations may cause more severe trauma. For students who have experienced trauma, the experience of attending school, focusing on coursework, and making friends is extremely difficult. This is because trauma can lead to feelings of intense grief, loss, and anxiety, along with physical symptoms that may range from nightmares and flashbacks to physical aches and pains, sleep problems, and appetite and weight problems.

RELATED RESOURCES

Movies

Spanglish (2004)—This film is about a single mother and her daughter, who immigrate to America in pursuit of a better life. The mother discovers that the culture in the United States challenges some of the values she wants to pass on to her daughter. The movie presents the clash between cultures, family values, and perspectives.

Entre Nos (2009)—This movie tells the story of a Colombian mother and her two children as they struggle to survive after her husband abandons them in New York to work in Miami. The story represents the immigrant experience of many who struggle to make it in a new country and hope for the American Dream to become a reality.

Amreeka (2009)—This film details the adventures and challenges of a single mother and her teenage son as they leave the West Bank and move in with their family in Illinois in search of a better future.

NOTES

1. Center for Applied Linguistics, "Secondary Newcomer Programs in the U.S.," www.cal.org/CALWebDB/newcomer/ (accessed April 4, 2010).

2. Internationals Network for Public Schools, "Our Schools," www.internationalsnps.org/our-schools/our-schools.html (accessed March 11, 2010).

3. Ameena Ghaffar-Kucher, "Citizenship and Belonging in the Age of Insecurity: Pakistani Immigrant Youth in New York City," in *Critical Approaches to Comparative Education: Vertical Case Studies from Africa, Europe, the Middle East and the Americas*, ed. Fran Vavrus and Lesley Bartlett (New York: Palgrave Macmillan, 2009), pp. 172–173.

4. Sonia Nieto, *Language, Culture, and Teaching: Critical Perspectives for a New Century* (Mahwah, NJ: Lawrence Erlbaum, 2002), p. 110.

7 A Multilingual America

"Neither of my parents speak English, and I am still struggling with the language. My brother and I have to always translate for my parents. I find translating for my parents frustrating sometimes, but on the other hand it also strengthens our relationship."

—Karen, China, 19 years old[1]

The United States is a land of many languages. Most immigrants come to this country speaking a language other than English. The high number of immigrants in the United States has helped to maintain high levels of linguistic diversity. Ideally, immigrants who come to this nation will have the opportunity to become bilingual and bicultural, and to function within and across two or more languages and cultures. Unfortunately, the rich multilingualism of our nation's newcomers has not always been welcomed or valued. A pressure to move toward English monolingualism for immigrants has resulted in the loss of many native languages. The views of the larger society can be seen in the policies put in place in schools across the country. This chapter looks more deeply into these difficult issues.

"I used to have a lot of problems with one of my teachers 'cause she didn't want us to talk Spanish in class and I thought that was like an insult to us, you know? Just telling us not to talk Spanish, 'cause [we] were Puerto Ricans . . . we're free to talk how we want."

—Marisol, Puerto Rico, 16 years old[2]

LANGUAGES OF THE UNITED STATES

Have you heard this joke before?

What do you call a person who speaks three languages? Trilingual
What do you call a person who speaks two languages? Bilingual
What do you call a person who speaks only one language?
  American

As this joke illustrates, the United States is often thought of as a monolingual English nation. However, the reality is actually quite different. Nearly one in five people (18 percent of the population) spoke a native language other than English in the year 2000, and over half of these people spoke Spanish. U.S. residents actually speak well over 300 languages.[3] The most commonly spoken languages in the United States, besides English, are Spanish, French, Chinese, German, Tagalog, Vietnamese, Italian, Korean, and Russian. The states with the highest number of languages spoken are California (207 languages), New York (169 languages), and Washington (163 languages), whereas South Dakota (62 languages), Vermont (64 languages), and Delaware (66 languages) have the least amount of linguistic diversity.[4] Some states have made an effort to accommodate their multilingual residents. For example, New Yorkers can purchase public transportation cards from machines in nine languages, and Kentuckians can take the written driver's license exam in one of twenty different languages. Our linguistic diversity is also evident in newspapers, TV channels, radio stations, and on the Internet.

A FOUNDATION OF MULTILINGUALISM

"They need to learn English instead of us learning their languages."
—Allison, United States, 17 years old

"A role in helping me to keep my native language was having Latino classmates, and because I think it is better to speak more languages than just one."
—Bryon, Ecuador, 16 years old

The Native Americans, the original inhabitants of the United States, spoke over 500 different languages. However, due to restrictive language policies imposed upon this group, coupled with strong pressures to leave their cultures behind, many languages have been lost. Currently there are approximately 150 Native American languages, from ten different language families, spoken in the United States. Native Americans laid the foundation for multilingualism in the nation, to which immigrants brought additional languages from all over the world.

In spite of many Native American languages already spoken in the nation, as well as the number of languages immigrants have brought with them to the United States, the push has been toward monolingualism. Unfortunately, languages other than English do not usually stay around very long. It often takes just two to three generations for a language to disappear from a family as it is replaced with English. That is, the children of immigrants often do not speak the family's home language, and if they do, their children generally do not.[5] This means that communication between immigrant grandparents and their grandchildren is often impossible. So, while immigrants represent the bulk of our bilingual citizens, their children and grandchildren generally become monolingual in English. As a result, most people are not able to speak two languages fluently, and they are not able to use these languages for professional purposes either. Thus, most bilinguals in the United States are immigrants or the children of immigrants. This differs from other nations, where bilingualism or multilingualism is the norm. Approximately one-half of the world is able to speak more than one language, but in the United States this rate drops to less than one-tenth.[6] And while much of the world does speak English, on a global scale we stand out as a country that lacks the ability to communicate, conduct business, and develop meaningful interactions in languages other than English.

In the United States, being bilingual is not equally valued, as we can see from the experiences of Mary and Miguel (see the sidebar called "A Tale of Two Bilinguals"). Generally, the prestige that bilinguals receive depends on the status of the languages they speak. Bilingual individuals are often placed into two categories: elective and circumstantial.[7] Elective bilinguals like Mary are usually U.S. born and White, come from a middle- to upper-class background, and grow up speaking English. During a point in their life they chose to acquire a second language through intensive language study, international travel, or work. Learning an additional language is more of a choice than a requirement for them, and they are frequently praised

A TALE OF TWO BILINGUALS

Mary was born to a White, middle-class family in a small town in Ohio. In high school she took Spanish classes but never really became fluent or comfortable in the language. In college she continued taking Spanish classes and her language ability increased. She was able to have basic conversations with people in stores and restaurants. Once she completed her undergraduate degree, she took a position working at a university in Mexico as an administrator. There, her Spanish flourished and she was easily able to communicate in personal and professional settings. After moving back to the United States to live and work, Mary had some opportunities to use her Spanish. Whenever she uses the language with anyone new, they always say something like, "Wow! Your Spanish is really good. Where did you learn it?" Mary is constantly put on a pedestal for being bilingual.

Miguel was born in Oaxaca, a state in southern Mexico. His first language was Mixtec, an indigenous language spoken by many in his community, but not by many people in other parts of Mexico. He started learning Spanish when he began school in Oaxaca. Miguel's family came to the United States when he was fourteen years old. He was placed in bilingual classes, where he was able to learn content in Spanish as he was learning English. Although Mixtec was never used in school, his family continued to speak the language at home. By the time Miguel graduated high school he was trilingual (Mixtec, Spanish, and English). However, when Miguel speaks, people focus on his English grammar and slightly accented English. Few people ask him about his ability to read and write in Spanish or to speak in Mixtec. Miguel's linguistic abilities are judged exclusively by his English skills.

for learning an additional language. On the other hand, circumstantial bilinguals like Miguel are often people of color who were born in another country or in the United States, and they are raised speaking a language other than English. In order to do well in school, get work, and complete day-to-day tasks, they must learn English. For this group, learning English is not a choice, and they are rarely praised for their ability to speak two languages. Therefore, while both groups may be able to function in two (or even three) languages, elective bilinguals are viewed as exceptional for their linguistic abilities while circumstantial bilinguals are often criticized for not speaking English well enough, and their bilingualism is often overlooked.

In spite of the push for English and only English, there are neighborhoods in the United States where multilingualism is alive and well. This can be seen through a community's

linguistic landscape—the public spaces where street signs, advertisements, and store signs are found in a variety of languages. These types of multilingual public displays go against the monolingual tide and show the value of other languages and the people who speak them.

BENEFITS OF BILINGUALISM

"All the time people think that since I am a Hispanic person, I don't speak English."

—Angela, Dominican Republic, 16 years old

Common sense tells us that speaking two languages is better than one. And speaking more than two languages is even better! There are many reasons that bilingualism is beneficial for individuals and societies. Four key benefits of being bilingual are presented here, although there are even more advantages to speaking, reading, writing, and understanding two or more languages.

Figure 7.1.   Multilingual storefronts in the diverse neighborhood of Jackson Heights in Queens, New York. Photo courtesy of Marko Kucher.

Flexible Thinking

Speaking a language has been referred to as a window to the world. If you are in a house with only one window, you

can still see your surroundings, but you will be limited in your perspective. However, if you have two or three or even four windows, what you see greatly expands. Therefore, speaking more than one language allows you to see things from a variety of cultural and linguistic perspectives. Also, being able to see that objects and concepts are not static, but that they change across languages, can increase mental flexibility. For example, for a monolingual English speaker, "water" is only that, whereas for a trilingual person it is also *dlo* in Haitian Creole and *eau* in French. As a result of understanding there is more than one way of saying or seeing things (beyond just specific words), bilingual individuals are able to see larger and more abstract ideas from multiple perspectives. Furthermore, they tend to be better at solving problems and more creative in their thinking.

Cross-Cultural Communication

When we speak a language we usually have an understanding of the culture in which it's spoken. So, bilinguals are also bicultural, which means they can comfortably function in settings with people from a variety of backgrounds. In addition to communicating with individuals from both of their language and cultural backgrounds, they are better able to appreciate and respect the values, social customs, and ways of viewing the world of people in both their communities. Even when bilinguals come into contact with individuals from a cultural group whose language they do not speak, they often have a better appreciation of differences. When people speak multiple languages they are likely to perceive differences as something to learn from as opposed to a problem that needs to be changed. In general, bilinguals appreciate the unique qualities between groups, instead of thinking of them as inferior.

Economic Opportunities

As the world is becoming more multilingual, there is a growing need for bilingual and biliterate employees. Employers are looking for people who can do more than just have casual

conversations in another language. They also need people
who can conduct professional conferences, write up reports,
and make decisions based on local cultures. Following the
9/11 attacks of 2001, the U.S. government has been actively
recruiting individuals who speak languages such as Farsi and
Arabic. One study of Latino bilinguals in three U.S. cities found
that they earned at least seven thousand dollars more per year
than those Latinos who only spoke English.[8] As an experiment,
explore the "help wanted" sections of any newspaper or
website. Do you notice ads for bilingual people? Which types
of jobs and languages are in demand? Bilinguals not only have
personal opportunities, but can also contribute to national
goals and the international economic system.

Transnational Identities

"What are you?" is a question frequently asked of people,
especially if they are an ethnic minority or speak English with a
"foreign" accent. Often the answer to this question is connected
to the languages a person speaks and the cultures with which they
feel connected. For bilingual people, identity is not exclusively
connected to one culture or one language. Nowadays many
people have transnational identities, meaning that the lines
of communication freely flow across countries, cultures, and
languages. Specifically, we have more opportunities to travel, live
abroad, and communicate via phone, e-mail, and the Internet.
Therefore, being bilingual allows people to create identities that
tie into all their cultural and linguistic backgrounds.

THE STATUS AND DEBATE AROUND
MAKING ENGLISH OFFICIAL

If you ask anyone, "What is the language of the United States?"
you will most likely hear that it is English. However, while
English is hands down the dominant language of the nation,
it is *not* the official language. When a language becomes
official it means that government must conduct all business
in that language. In spite of pressure from some groups in

the United States to mandate English (only) as the country's official language, the United States has not adopted an official language. But even in the absence of a national English policy, over half of the country's states have made English their official language. This has had the effect of removing services such as translation and the availability of documents in immigrants' native languages, as well as reducing the number of bilingual programs in public schools. For example, the state of Arizona has adopted English as its official language. This measure poses a challenge to newly arrived immigrants and Native Americans[9] alike. The debates around language officialization push us to consider whether we want to be a country that promotes monolingualism or moves toward multilingualism, in step with the majority of the globalizing world.

There are a range of organizations in the United States that are committed to changing the nation's laws to make English the official language. One such group's position statement and actions for moving toward this goal are as follows:

> ProEnglish is the nation's leading advocate of official English. We work through the courts and in the court of public opinion to defend English's historic role as America's common, unifying language, and to persuade lawmakers to adopt English as the official language at all levels of government.

Agenda for Action

- Adopting laws or constitutional amendments declaring English the official language of the United States, and of individual states.
- Defending the right of individual states to make English the official language of government operations.
- Ending bilingual education (e.g., foreign language immersion) programs in public schools.
- Repealing federal mandates for the translation of government documents and voting ballots into languages other than English.
- Opposing the admission of territories as states unless they have adopted English as their official language.[10]

Some people believe that those who favor English-only policies do so because of their fear not only of differences in terms of language, but also of the increased cultural and racial diversity in our nation. They are threatened by the way our nation is changing from a predominantly White- and English-dominant nation to one that is more Brown and Black and multilingual. For example, political scientist Samuel Huntington wrote that Mexicans pose the greatest threat to the "American" culture and language, whereby we could become a nation of two divided languages (English and Spanish) and two divided cultures (Anglo-Protestant and Hispanic).[11]

Most groups that oppose the use of languages other than English in public settings do so because they claim that speaking different languages will pose a threat to national unity. The United States has heard these arguments before, since citizens expressed similar beliefs during the increase in European and specifically German-speaking immigrants in the 1700s and 1800s. Reacting to the increased German immigration in 1750, Benjamin Franklin wrote, "Pennsylvania would become a German colony; instead of learning our language, we must learn theirs, or live as in a foreign country."[12] Nearly three hundred years later we can see that the status of the English language is firmly in place. This example demonstrates that other languages have always existed in our nation, and that they have actually posed no threat to English. Over time, the main changes that have taken place are simply the languages and countries of origin of our newest immigrant groups.

Generally, the attitudes that people hold about different languages are not about the actual languages, but are really about the people who speak those languages. The stigma of bilingualism aims to build upon a fear of other languages or differences.[13] English-only policies that are proposed are less about actual languages and more about the people who speak the languages. Therefore, racism, linguicism (the discrimination of people based on their languages), and xenophobia (the fear of people from other countries) are actually at the heart of English-only mandates that aim to squash the languages and identities of immigrants. Rather than creating a both/and situation where immigrants can hold onto their native language and learn English, the pressure is to move toward English only, putting immigrants in a position where they are forced to give up their bilingual and bicultural advantages.

Over time, there have been several proposals to amend the Constitution in order to make English the official language of the United States. In 1982, Senator Samuel Ichiye Hayakawa was the first to advocate for such a law. Many others have tried to pass similar amendments, but until now, they have not been successful. Nevertheless, the efforts continue, most recently when U.S. Representative Stephen King from Iowa introduced the National Language Act of 2009. We will have to watch to see whether the federal government will follow in the path of the majority of its states that have already made English the official language, or whether the United States will remain a nation without a designated official language.

In spite of the status of English in the United States, its importance in the international arena continues to rise. The prevalence of English can be seen in the increasing number of children and adults studying English in public

---

PRESIDENT OBAMA'S VIEW ON ENGLISH-ONLY LAWS AND BILINGUALISM

I don't understand when people are going around worrying about, "We need to have English only." They want to pass a law, "We need to have English only." Now, I agree that immigrants should learn English. I agree with that. But understand this, instead of worrying about whether immigrants can learn English—they'll learn English—you need to make sure your child can speak Spanish. You should be thinking about, how can your child become bilingual? We should have every child speaking more than one language. It's embarrassing when Europeans come over here, they all speak English, they speak French, they speak German. And then we go over to Europe and all we can say [is] "merci beaucoup," right?

—Speech made by President Obama on July 8, 2008, during a campaign stop in Powder Springs, Georgia[14]

and private schools, the rise in publications of English as a
Foreign Language, and the use of English across business
and government sectors. Some have referred to English as the
lingua franca, a term that refers to a common language used in
diplomacy, international business, and technology. Worldwide,
over 500 million people speak English. And as the spread of
English continues throughout the world, many people question
whether the United States really needs to give the language
official status in the nation. Clearly, English is a powerful
language that continues to dominate on the national and global
scale. At this point in time there is no country that designates
English as its only official language. English is an official
language in nations such as South Africa, Canada, and India,
but there are other official languages in these countries as well.
In this way, these countries remain bilingual nations and can
continue to provide protections for speakers of other languages.

SCHOOL PROGRAMS FOR IMMIGRANTS LEARNING ENGLISH

*"[Starting first grade in the United States] was scary
because they put me in a monolingual class. . . . My
mom said it was for me to learn English faster, but it
was hard 'cause I didn't know nothing. . . . Everything
was English and I'm like . . . what am I doing?"*
—Cassia, Venezuela, 18 years old

Learning a new language is a difficult task that generally takes
many years. It can take anywhere from one to three years
to learn a language for basic day-to-day communication.
However, learning a language for academic proficiency takes
much longer. In other words, developing the ability to write
an essay about a historical time period, conduct and write up a
scientific experiment, or debate the effects of global warming
in a second language takes more time. Most estimates say that
developing that kind of language ability can take anywhere
from three to ten years.[15] The time depends on a variety of
factors, including education level and literacy skills in the native
language, motivation, and quality of instruction.

125

When immigrant students enter U.S. schools, they must learn several things: a new culture, a new language, and—at the same time—content in the subject areas. In order to support students who need to learn English, a variety of options are available to immigrants who enter kindergarten through twelfth grade public schools. Because of an important court case in San Francisco in 1974 (*Lau v. Nichols*), all schools must offer assistance during the school day to students learning English. The choices vary from state to state. They range from bilingual education, in which subjects are taught in both English and the native language, to English as a Second Language (ESL) programs, where students receive additional help with English during the school day. It is illegal for schools to place English learners into general mainstream classrooms without any support. This type of education has been called "sink or swim," because it was as if students were thrown into deep water and left on their own, to either float (attain English on their own) or to drown academically. Some students did learn to "swim" in that way, but most did not. Fortunately, this type of educational program is no longer an option in U.S. public schools.

Bilingual education programs are a less common—but very effective—way of helping immigrant students learn English, master grade level content, and develop their native language too. These programs generally have one of the following two goals:

1. **Subtractive bilingual programs use the native language to help students keep up in content areas such as math, social studies, and science while they are learning English. As soon as the school feels the student's English ability is on grade level, the student moves into classes where English is the only language of instruction. In this type of program, the native language is used as a bridge, which is later removed as instruction moves to all English, thereby subtracting the students' home language.**

2. **Additive bilingual programs aim to develop students' English as they continue to develop the native language so that students can be both bilingual and biliterate. These programs use the native language and English for an extended period of time, regardless of a student's level of English. Students often enter these programs speaking only their native language, but**

after many years in the program are able to read, write, and complete math, science, and social studies assignments in both languages. Therefore, the program adds on another language.

Bilingual programs may take many different forms. Some spend more time in the native language, especially when students are in the early stages of learning English. Others are careful to divide time equally between the two languages. In high schools, students in bilingual programs may have some subjects taught in English and others in their native language, or a teacher of one subject may switch between languages. Not only do bilingual programs offer immigrant students a chance to learn in their native language, they also allow students the opportunity to be in a class where the students and teachers understand their culture and can help them become both bilingual and bicultural.

While bilingual programs have many advantages, their existence and effectiveness have often been challenged. Political pressures have caused states such as California, Massachusetts, and Arizona to pass measures to ban bilingual education. This is in spite of research that has proven that high quality bilingual programs are the best programs for English learners.[16]

Even in states where bilingual education is still an option, the availability of bilingual programs often depends on the number of students who speak a given language and the presence of bilingual teachers. If either of these is lacking, schools must then provide ESL programs. Just like bilingual education, ESL also varies in the way it is put into practice. Some schools have a special ESL class where students who speak a variety of languages come together for one to three periods a day to receive instruction in the English language. Another option is for the ESL teacher to "push in" to other classes and work with the content teachers to provide students with English support as they complete the regular coursework. While ESL is helpful for students to learn English, it does not usually provide opportunities for students to use or develop their native language.

Regardless of the type of programs available for English learners, most students will also be required to take a "foreign language" class, either in middle or high school. Some schools may only have one language whereas others may offer choices ranging from Spanish to Mandarin to Latin, to name a few. The courses vary by individual school district and depend on funding, interests, and demographics. These classes were primarily designed for students who have not had exposure to the language of study before. For immigrants who are already proficient in a different first language, foreign language classes can be a disappointment. Often they are very easy for native speakers. Therefore, two choices are available to avoid such situations: (1) Students can see if a heritage language or Advanced Placement (AP) language or literature class is available instead. Heritage language classes are created for students who already speak the language at home and need support in advanced reading and writing skills. (2) Another option is to take a course in a different language. While this will be a challenge, when one is already bilingual, adding another language is often easier, especially if the languages are related in their grammar, writing system, and vocabulary.

Although it is clear that the United States has an enormous resource in its speakers of over three hundred languages, our nation has not yet determined how to support and benefit from the multilingualism of its people.

OPPOSITION TO DIFFERENCE: MY STORY

My family came to the United States when I was nearly six years old. We arrived as religious refugees who were granted permission to leave what is now Latvia and what in the 1980s was still the Soviet Union. Our family was one of tens of thousands of Soviet Jews who sought to escape the anti-Jewish, or anti-Semitic, views that limited economic and social opportunities for Jews, as well as their religious freedoms. I recall that when we arrived in the apartment provided to us by a Jewish social service agency in Columbus, Ohio, I quickly became friends with two girls who had just moved from Israel. In their apartment we played Memory and I repeated the words "yes" and "no," the only English I knew at the time.

After only a few months of attending U.S. schools, I began to understand that English was the language that mattered and speaking other languages was looked down upon. After a few short months, I refused to utter a word of Russian to my family. They spoke to me in Russian and I answered in English. I remember how embarrassed I felt when my mom dared to speak Russian to me in any public place, or worse yet, in front of my friends. Speaking another language and coming from a different country was a secret I tried very hard to conceal. Over time my English improved (although I always had trouble with reading and writing), and my Russian worsened to the point that words would not come to me easily or at all. It was not until my college years where I had the option of taking Russian courses that I saw that having been born in another country and growing up speaking a different language was actually an advantage. The classes I took were intended for students learning the language for the first time. I did quite well in the classes and learned to read and write Russian a bit (though it's still a slow process!). Since then I have interviewed for a job where Russian was required, and I think one reason I was not offered the position was because my Russian abilities were so limited. As I look back on my history as a bilingual person, I feel fortunate that I have not completely lost my native language, but I also believe that society pushed me to assimilate toward English monolingualism through hidden messages about the superiority of English. Now I see that true superiority lies in speaking many languages as well as developing an understanding of the cultures they come from.

RELATED RESOURCES

Book

Do You Speak American? by Robert MacNeil and William Cran (New York: Random House, 2004)—This book allows readers to explore the diversity of the English language as it appears in different regions of the nation (see the accompanying website in the next section).

Websites

Do You Speak American?, PBS, www.pbs.org/speak/—This website goes with the book by the same title.

Living Tongues: Institute for Endangered Languages, www. livingtongues.org/—This website provides information about the world's languages that are in danger of becoming extinct. Related books and websites are provided, as is information about the dying languages.

U.S. English, www.us-english.org— This is the website of an organization devoted to enacting legislation that would make English the official language of the United States. Information about the group's mission, prior efforts to amend the Constitution, and recent news about language laws and policies are available.

Movie

Speaking in Tongues (2010), by Patchwork Films—This documentary follows the journey of four students from elementary to middle school in U.S. public schools as they become bilingual. Through their stories issues of individual and national identity, immigration, and globalization are explored.

NOTES

1. "Immigrations: Making New Americans," *Teen Voices* 7, no. 2 (Summer 1998), p. 21.

2. Sonia Nieto, *Language, Culture, and Teaching: Critical Perspectives for a New Century* (Mahwah, NJ: Lawrence Erlbaum, 2002), p. 128.

3. U.S. Census Bureau, "Language Use and English Speaking Ability: 2000," 2000, www.census.gov/prod/2003pubs/c2kbr-29.pdf (accessed November 28, 2009).

4. Modern Language Association Data Center, "Most Spoken Languages in the Entire US in 2005," www.mla.org/map_data&dcwindow=new (accessed December 24, 2008).

5. Joshua Fishman, *Reversing Language Shift: Theoretical and Empirical Foundations of Assistance to Threatened Languages* (Clevedon, UK: Multilingual Matters, 1991), p. 287.

6. Associated Press, "USA Way Behind in Languages: Half of Europe's Citizens Know 2 Languages," Breitbart, 2005, www .breitbart.com/article.php?id=D8CQJUE02&show_article=1 (accessed January 5, 2010).

7. Colin Baker, *Foundations of Bilingual Education and Bilingualism*, 4th ed. (Clevedon, UK: Multilingual Matters, 2006), pp. 4–5.

8. James Crawford and Stephen Krashen, *English Learners in American Classrooms: 101 Questions, 101 Answers* (New York: Scholastic, 2007), p. 31.

9. Arizona is home to twenty-one distinct federally recognized tribes, making Native people an important voting block and potential swing vote in the state. English-only laws have prevented elderly Native Americans who speak only their Native language from receiving election ballots in their own languages, thereby making it difficult for any individual who is not fluent in English to participate in the nation's democratic system.

10. ProEnglish, "Mission," www.proenglish.org/index. php?option=com_content&view=article&id=46&Itemid=54&lang= en (accessed October 20, 2010).

11. Samuel Huntington, *Who Are We? The Challenge to America's National Identity* (New York: Simon & Schuster, 2004), pp. 221–256.

12. Bill Ong Hing, *Defining America through Immigration Policy* (Philadelphia, PA: Temple University Press, 2004), p. 3.

13. James Crawford, *Educating English Learners: Language Diversity in the Classroom*, 5th ed. (Los Angeles, CA: Bilingual Educational Services, 2004), p. 133.

14. President Barack Obama, Address, Powder Springs, GA July 8, 2008, www.salon.com/technology/how_the_world_ works/2008/07/08/bilingual_obama (accessed December 20, 2009).

15. Jim Cummins, "Language Development and Academic Learning," in *Language, Culture, and Cognition*, ed. Lilliam Malevé and Georges Duquette (Clevedon, UK: Multilingual Matters, 1991), pp. 161–175.

16. Wayne Thomas and Virginia Collier, "A National Study of School Effectiveness for Language Minority Students' Long-Term Academic Achievement," *CREDE*, 2002, www.usc.edu/dept/ education/CMMR/CollierThomasComplete.pdf (accessed November 18, 2009).

8 Encountering Discrimination

Although the United States offers immigrants opportunities beyond those available in their home countries, many also face discrimination based on their backgrounds. There are a range of groups in the United States who are discriminated against based on their race, language and immigrant status, to name just a few of the areas that people use to mistreat others. Although discrimination in the United States is not just directed at immigrant groups, they are certainly a population that must deal with its negative impacts. However, it should be noted that discrimination is not a one-way street; discrimination occurs among immigrant groups as well as between immigrant groups and U.S.-born individuals. In spite of the broad reach of discrimination, this chapter will focus on how immigrants experience and deal with discrimination in the United States.

While anyone can be discriminated against, the groups that face discrimination on a regular basis are those who are "minoritized." Unlike the word *minority*, which you may be familiar with, *minoritized* refers to a group that has been placed in a lower position socially, economically, or politically, but has the ability to change its status (although this is not easy or quick).[1] In the United States minoritized groups are those who do not fit within the majority or mainstream. That means people who are not U.S. born, White, Christian, male, native-English speaking, middle-upper class, and heterosexual likely fit into a group that has faced discrimination, although to different degrees. Those people who fit into the categories above do not make up a numerical majority of the U.S. population;

"When I first arrived there were many students who were making fun of my accent. When I say I am from Uzbekistan they are like very ignorant because they didn't know the country so they are mixing it up with Pakistan and things like this. They also say that I am from Japan. That makes me feel upset because I didn't know that I would be treated this way when I came here."

—Alisher, Uzbekistan, 16 years old

133

however, they hold the majority of the power when it comes to government, business, and wealth. As a result, minoritized groups have been placed and held in a position of inferiority through discrimination by those who hold privileges due to their economic status, race, gender, or other differences. Those in the majority can enjoy the benefits that come with power, at the expense of others.

INDIVIDUAL, INSTITUTIONAL, AND CULTURAL DISCRIMINATION

Discrimination, especially when it is connected with race, language, religion, or other human and social differences, is the process by which people are treated in unjust and different ways because of specific aspects of their background.[2] Scholars who have studied the topic believe that it occurs on three different levels. The first level, *individual*, is what people think of most often when it comes to discrimination. This is when someone is on the receiving end of something as small as a look or a rude comment, or as large as being yelled at or physically abused because of his or her background. Individual discrimination can occur in a one-on-one setting, or it can be a group of people against an individual or a group. Examples of individual discrimination could range from references to a Jew as cheap to compliments on an African American's eloquent English to a person being beat up because he or she looks gay.

The second type of discrimination, *institutional*, presents itself in organizational settings such as schools, government, law enforcement, and housing/real estate. Unlike individual discrimination, that which occurs on the institutional level has a long-lasting and negative impact on larger groups of minoritized people. Examples of institutional discrimination include the severity of punishments, such as prison sentences, that Black and Latino people receive in comparison to White individuals; the way potential Black and Latino home buyers or renters are steered away from living in mostly White neighborhoods; and the academic achievement gap, where White and Asian students outperform those from Latino and

Black backgrounds when it comes to standardized testing scores and high school graduation rates. Although the reasons for these educational differences are complex, they include abundance or lack of resources/funding available to schools in racially segregated communities, culturally biased tests that favor knowledge associated with the mainstream, a mismatch between the culture of schools and of students' homes, and teachers' attitudes toward and expectations of the different racial and ethnic groups.

The last category of discrimination, *cultural*, relates to the areas such as languages, the arts, literature, and music. Basically, any area that is valued by the mainstream culture—such as standard or academic English, classical European music, and ballet—is valued while anything considered outside of the dominant group is devalued. Cultural discrimination occurs when workers are told they are only allowed to speak in English or when schools favor events such as a Beethoven concert over Salsa or Bhangra performances. These three levels of discrimination make life for immigrants even more challenging as they work to acclimate themselves to a new culture, language, and country.

In the United States individuals and groups experience discrimination based on many reasons, too many to go into here. This chapter will discuss four types of discrimination that are especially relevant to immigrant communities in the United States: racism, linguicism, religious discrimination, and xenophobia.

Racism

Even though the United States elected its first multiracial president in 2008, the nation is still struggling to move beyond its racist past and present. In the United States race is an area that is highly controversial and even taboo, as many people feel uncomfortable having open and honest conversations about it. Although scientists have proven there is no such thing as race to be found in a human's genetic makeup,[3] the concept of race is widely used as a way to make (false) judgments about people.

When people talk about race, they are generally referring to a person's phenotype. This means the color or tone of their skin, their hair texture, and the size and shape of their facial features. People's intelligence, attractiveness, and athleticism are often tied to the racial group it is believed they belong to.

When it comes to race, there is a need to sort people into distinct categories or boxes, similar to those people check off when filling out a form. The five major racial groups in the nation, from largest to smallest, are White, Latino/Hispanic, Black, Asian, and Native American. You may have noticed that while the White and Black categories are based on color, Asian, Latino, and Native American are categories based on the part of the world the individuals or their ancestors come from. Multiracial individuals who fit into more than one group, such as President Obama, are often forced to either select one category that they identify with more closely or become part of the group referred to as "Other."

Each racial group, with the exception of Native Americans, includes both people who are immigrants and people who are U.S. born. When it comes to the foreign born, White people are mostly thought of as coming from European countries. Black people include immigrants from Caribbean and African nations. Latinos come from all over Latin America, while Asians emigrate from over fifty vast and diverse nations. While these are generalizations about which nations and continents immigrants from each racial group come from, it is important to remember that people of each racial group live in nearly every part of the world. Therefore, one can never assume which part of the world a person comes from based on his or her race.

Immigrants often find that the racial group they belonged to in their country of origin no longer is the same group they are considered to be a part of in the United States. For example, in Argentina, Milagros was White. However, when she came to Massachusetts for college, all of a sudden she realized she was no longer viewed as White, but as a Latina. The same is also true for people from the Dominican Republic, who in their home country consider themselves Latino, but after they land on U.S. soil are often thought of as Black. This fluid nature of race shows that it is a concept that is not scientific, but based on one's location and the ways race is perceived there. Thus, just as one's racial group changes when he or she crosses borders, so, too, do the associations and stereotypes that are connected with being a part of a racial category.

In the United States those with darker skin tones experience racism in a variety of ways, from subtle to severe. Many immigrant teens and adolescents face or witness instances of racism in their schools, communities, and society at large.

"Most people in the United States think Latinos are in gangs. But that's not true. We're here because we want to study."
—Ricardo, Mexico, 18 years old

"I feel there is still a lot of racism, and I just do not understand why people hate others just because of their color or because we can't speak good English. I think the U.S. needs to give a chance to immigrants because we all come here to do better."
—Berthe, Haiti, 16 years old

"In sixth grade I was in advanced courses. I had a math teacher who did not want me to go on to advanced math and science in seventh grade. I did not understand why because I had gotten As in her classes and I thought I was like everyone else who had gotten As and was going on to advanced class. I just got this feeling that she did not think that I was going to succeed, but I was like, how am I any different from any of your other students? At that point everybody else in the class was White and I was the only Mexican."
—Martin, U.S.-Mexico Transnational, 22 years old

Linguicism

The term *linguicism* refers to the way people are (mis) treated or viewed as less than because of the language(s)

⊚⊚⊚⊚⊚⊚⊚⊚⊚⊚⊚⊚⊚⊚⊚⊚⊚⊚⊚⊚⊚⊚⊚

THE MODEL MINORITY MYTH

"When you get bad grades, people look at you really strangely because you are sort of distorting the way they see an Asian."
—An Asian American high school student[4]

While most groups of color must endure negative stereotypes, there is a group that stands out as an exception: Asians. In the United States, immigrants and native-born citizens of Asian descent are labeled as the "model minority." This means that when it comes to all the minoritized groups, Asians are viewed as the most successful and touted as role models for other groups, who should aim to achieve the status of Asian groups. Embedded in this stereotype is the belief that Asians do well in school, are especially strong in math, and tend to be studious, respectful of authority, and play musical instruments such as the piano or string instruments. While there are people of Asian descent that certainly fit within some of these descriptions, there are significant problems when all Asians are expected to live up to these stereotypes, even though the stereotypes place them in a positive light.

The model minority myth may actually be more hurtful than helpful for Asians as well as other minoritized groups for a variety of reasons. First, this stereotype is questionable because it takes the diverse category of "Asians" and makes them one homogenous, or similar, group. If we look at who is considered Asian, we find that this term includes 4 billion people from more than fifty countries that range from Afghanistan to China to Thailand to Yemen. In addition to country of origin, Asians also vary in terms of their socioeconomic class. A study in the United States found that Chinese-American children from middle-class families performed much better in schools than those from poor families, a situation that can be found across other ethnic and racial groups too. The reasons are related to the resources and support middle- to upper-class families can offer their children, such as being able to help them with schoolwork due to their higher levels of formal education, being able to afford tutoring and other enrichment activities, and having more time to spend with their children (as opposed to working many hours or jobs).[5] It is not due to any connections between intelligence and income level. Furthermore, the model minority myth overlooks that certain Asian groups have low levels of high school completion. The 2000 census found that of the Cambodian, Hmong, and Laotians in the United States over the age of twenty-five, less than half graduated from high school. Finally, the model minority stereotype is problematic because it allows people to believe that one's racial and ethnic background is connected with one's intelligence, or lack of it. The stereotype is harmful to Black and Latino groups who are constantly being compared to Asians, just as it is to Asians themselves who may fear asking for help in school if they are not doing well because of the perception that they are supposed to excel in all areas of academics.[6] For all these reasons, the model minority myth is one that should be questioned and challenged, similar to other stereotypes placed upon this and other minoritized groups.

they speak, and those they do not speak. In the United States English is not the official language of the country (currently one does not exist), but it is without a doubt the language of power.[7] Therefore, people who do not speak English are looked down upon, even if they speak two, three, or four other languages. Just speaking English is not enough to escape linguicism, as one must speak a valued variety of English, which in the United States is referred to as standard or academic English. It is often associated with middle-upper class White people, although it is spoken by individuals from many groups. For immigrants who come to the United States speaking languages other than English, most eventually learn to speak English, to different degrees. Those who come to the country after they've gone through puberty and did not have opportunities to learn the language in their home country often speak English with an accent that differs from people who grew up speaking the language. While immigrants who come from France, England, or Italy are viewed as having "smart" or "sophisticated" accents when they speak English, those who come from Mexico, Haiti, or China are looked down upon for their accented English. Even immigrants who come from countries where English is spoken or who have learned to speak a non-American variety of English (such as Trinidadian or Jamaican English) may find they are victims of linguicism in the United States. For example, it has been the case that immigrant students from English-speaking Caribbean nations have been placed in ESL (English as a Second Language) classes, mainly due to their accents. Such courses are specifically designed for students who grew up speaking a different language and started learning English in U.S. schools. ESL is not for students for whom English is a language they grew up speaking. This situation demonstrates how people are instantly judged by the accent with which they speak English, some being perceived as educated and worldly while others are viewed as uneducated and poor, simply for the way they sound.

Linguicism, just like other forms of discrimination, goes beyond the ways people are perceived to how they are treated. Thus, people may find themselves in a position where they must constantly explain where they come from, experience difficulty finding jobs because they are viewed as less intelligent, or face bans on speaking their native language in public places. See the teen quotes below for instances in which Spanish-speaking immigrant teens have experienced discrimination either because they don't speak English or they speak it with an accent that marks them as foreign born.

"A common stereotype is that Spanish [speaking] people talk bad about English [speaking] people when we are among them. It makes me feel really uncomfortable because it's a serious lie."
—Estefan, Venezuela, 17 years old

"As a Latino immigrant and bilingual student, I have been discriminated against a bunch of times in school. . . . [Once] the physical education teacher was there talking to some white students. One girl he was speaking to said out loud, 'I don't want to talk about it in front of them,' pointing to me and my friend. The teacher replied, 'Don't worry. They probably don't even speak English!' And they both started laughing at us."
—Alejandro, Mexico, 16 years old[8]

Religious Discrimination

The United States has traditionally been thought of as a nation founded on Christian values, in spite of the fact that the First Amendment of the U.S. Constitution requires the separation of church (or religion) and state. In theory, this means that the nation should be neutral in terms of religion, and decisions made by the government and other public institutions such as schools or courts should not be based on the religious beliefs of any group. Furthermore, the United

PUNISHED FOR SPEAKING SPANISH

Zack Rubio is a typical high school junior in a diverse blue-collar community in Kansas City, Kansas.[9] He is the son of Mexican American immigrants and is bilingual in English and Spanish. On a regular school day in 2005 during free time when Zack was outside of the classroom a peer asked him, "¿Me prestas un dolar?" (Will you lend me a dollar?), to which he responded in Spanish "No problema" (No problem). A staff member overheard this interaction and sent Zack to the principal's office. There he was reprimanded for speaking Spanish in school and given a day and half of suspension. It was only after his father came to the school to demand to see proof of a policy against speaking languages other than English on school grounds that the punishment was dropped. This case is not unique, as other students have been punished for using their native language in school. Beyond educational settings, people have been reprimanded for speaking other languages in the workplace and on school buses.

Some questions to consider:

◎ **Do you think Zack or any other student should be punished for speaking a language other than English in school?**
◎ **In your school experiences, do teachers allow bilingual students to use their native languages in the classroom? Do you feel this is a positive or negative practice?**
◎ **How does limiting people's right to speak languages impact their civil rights, such as freedom of speech?**

States has been a nation to which people have come from all over the world in search of religious freedom, as they were persecuted for practicing their religion elsewhere. Immigrants in the United States seeking to openly and freely practice their religions range from the Puritans from England in the 1600s, to Jews from all over Europe who came during the World War II era and beyond, to most recently Falun Gong practitioners from China.

While the United States has traditionally been a place to which minoritized religious groups from all over the world have escaped, not all groups have found the country to be a welcoming place. This is especially the case for Muslims following the events of September 11, 2001. Since the extremist group Al Qaeda, which claims to operate on behalf of Muslim interests (an idea most Muslims would contest), was linked to the deaths of thousands of people on U.S. soil, many people and organizations across the nation have turned against Muslims, as well as those who are perceived to be a part of the group. Although it was a small extremist subgroup who were involved in the tragic events of 9/11, Muslims have often taken the blame and, as a result, have been discriminated against because of the actions of a few. The perception of Muslims as dangerous and unpatriotic has been reinforced by the media since the 9/11 attacks. News reports sometimes fail to distinguish between extremist terrorist groups and the larger Muslim community, who are equally opposed to such actions and beliefs.

Ameena Ghaffar-Kucher has used the term "religification" to describe the way Muslims are viewed by others as well as themselves, particularly since the 9/11 era of "increased suspicion and surveillance of individuals from the Middle East and South Asia."[10] Muslims have come to be perceived as outsiders, terrorists, and anti-American by many outside of their group. They are seen mostly through the lens of their religion, with little attention paid to their race, ethnicity, or country of origin. Perhaps as a result of the way they are viewed by others, many Muslims in the United States have come to self-identify primarily through their religion, regardless of whether they practice it or not. Therefore, while Muslims are viewed by others and themselves through this one aspect of their identity, there is a difference: within the group, there is a positive association of the term that allows for a sense of community and safety, while for many outside the group, negative stereotypes dominate the way Muslims are viewed.

Among Muslims, Pakistanis are the largest immigrant group living in the United States.[11] In one study of Pakistani American high school youth, every student mentioned that since the 9/11 attacks each had been called a terrorist at one point in school.

"My school experience was pretty good before 9/11. However, in sixth grade, after 9/11, I have been looked [at] as a stereotype. Everybody used to call me a terrorist. All through junior high school, people used to call me Osama or Saddam."

—Latif, Pakistan, 15 years old[12]

"Now we just joke about it. We'll be like, 'get away from us, or we'll bomb you . . .' You know how you make a joke out of stuff because it bothers you but you don't want to show that it bothers you."

—Anonymous, U.S.-born Pakistani high school student[13]

SIKHS: MISTAKEN AND UNDER ATTACK

Like Muslims who have faced discrimination in the United States, individuals of the Sikh religion, many of whom are descendants from Punjab, India, have also faced a similar backlash since 9/11. Although Sikhism is a religion that is not associated with the Muslim faith, its followers have been wrongly associated with it. This misconception is likely due to the turbans worn by men who practice the Sikh religion. The lack of awareness of the different religions and customs they each follow has resulted in many Sikh Americans being victimized by verbal and physical assaults. There have even been murders of Sikh men simply because they were perceived to be Muslims.[14] Sikh institutions have also been vandalized. A *Gurdwara* (a Sikh place of worship) in Fresno, California, was defaced with the words "It's not your country" spray-painted on the outside gate. This is despite the fact that many Sikhs in the community were U.S. born, and those who were immigrants are very much a part of the country, where they work, pay taxes, and raise their families.[15] Since 9/11 hundreds of cases of discrimination against Sikhs have been reported across the United States as they are often misidentified as Muslim, and as terrorists, or people who support terrorism.

Xenophobia

"We are all equal. We are people, not different from each other—coming from another country does not make me better than you. Because I'm from Haiti and you from the U.S. does not make you a better person. We have the same rights, freedom of speech; we are equal, we are human beings."

—Elsie, Haiti, 15 years old

"They [teachers] wonder why sometimes we [immigrants] don't seem interested in school. The fact is school isn't that interested in us."

—Alejandro, Mexico, 16 years old[16]

The fear or dislike of those who are foreign or different is referred to as xenophobia (pronounced "zenophobia"). It is often directed at immigrants, but can also be experienced by people who look different or foreign, based on their race, language(s), or attire. It is ironic that while nearly everyone currently living in the United States is either an immigrant themselves or had ancestors who immigrated to the country, hatred of the most recent immigrant groups persists. The nation's short-term memory of its rich immigration history has resulted in the continual discrimination of immigrants over the centuries. Although it may be hard to imagine, the xenophobia many Latinos face in the United States today is similar to that experienced by German immigrants in the 1700s when they were turned away from rooming houses, or what Irish immigrants experienced in the mid-1800s when they would see job ads which specified that Irish people need not apply.[17] Xenophobia has always been present in the United States. The only aspect that has changed is the groups it has been aimed at.

Although no group is immune to xenophobia, Latinos who are both immigrants and U.S.-born have been victims of an increasing number of hate crimes due to their (perceived) immigrant status. There are a variety of reasons (see chapter 3 for additional information) that may lead people to discriminate against Latinos:

144

- They are the largest minority group in the nation, and they continue to grow in numbers, which contributes to a fear that those in power will lose their position as America becomes more brown and more Spanish speaking.
- Latinos are blamed for taking "American" jobs.
- Latinos are viewed as criminals because they are perceived as coming to the country illegally.

While these beliefs are often false, it has not stopped the increasing rate of hate crimes against Latinos in the United States. The FBI first started using the term *hate crimes* in the 1980s (although the concept has always existed) to refer to acts of violence committed against an individual or group because of race, ethnicity, gender, sexual orientation, religion, or disability. The rate of hate crimes against Latinos has been on the rise since 2003, whereas the number of crimes against other groups (such as African Americans, women, or Jews) has either remained the same or decreased.[18] In 2006 Hispanics suffered the highest number of hate crimes related to ethnicity or nationality in the nation, with over 60 percent of all such crimes.[19] The rise in crimes can be connected to the anti-immigration feelings that have swept through the nation, affecting not only Latin American immigrants, but people who simply look like they may be a part of this group. Xenophobia has impacted not only Latinos born outside of the United States, but also those who are U.S.-born and naturalized citizens.

RELATED RESOURCES

Book

Mexican Whiteboy, by Matt de la Peña (New York: Random House, 2008)—This fictional story features Danny Lopez, a biracial teen born to Mexican and White parents. As Danny, a talented baseball player, moves between schools and neighborhoods, he deals with the feelings of being an outsider.

145

IMMIGRATION-RELATED HATE CRIMES

Hate crimes against Latinos have been taking place across the country and are making national headlines. Here are two incidents that took place at the hands of teenagers with strong anti-Mexican and anti-immigrant views:

- In 2007 four current and former high school football players in the mining town of Shenandoah, Pennsylvania, attacked Luis Ramirez. Luis, a twenty-five-year-old Mexican immigrant and father of two, was severely beaten by the group. While being kicked in the head, the teens yelled, "This is Shenandoah, this is America, go back to Mexico!" Luis died after two days in a coma as a result of the injuries from the attack. Following a trial, two of the teens were found guilty of simple assault, but were cleared of the more serious charges of murder, aggravated assault, and ethnic intimidation. Another teen pleaded guilty to violating Luis' civil rights while the fourth was still facing charges in juvenile court.[20]

- In the Long Island, New York, town of Pathchogue, a group of teens made a habit of going out and finding Mexicans to assault. They named this activity "beaner jumping." When questioned by police, one youth explained, "I don't go out doing this very often, maybe once a week." One evening Carlos Orellana, an Ecuadorian construction worker, was told to "Go back to Mexico" as he was robbed by a gang of teenagers on bicycles and beaten until he was unconscious. Other such incidents had occurred in the town, creating a pattern of crimes against those believed to be Mexicans. However, police and town officials did not act to address the underlying anti-immigrant feelings overtaking the town. Then on November 8, 2008, an incident occurred that finally brought the issue to the forefront of community, state, and nation. A group of youth, all sixteen or seventeen years old, attacked, stabbed, and killed a thirty-seven-year-old Ecuadorian immigrant named Marcello Lucero.[21]

In order to stop hate crimes such as those related to xenophobic attitudes toward Latinos, it is not enough to simply punish those who committed the crime. Without addressing stereotypes that are held against immigrant groups (and others) through education that involves learning the facts and open dialogue, hate crimes will only continue to occur and grow in severity and numbers.

Website

Hate: Crossing the Line (2009), a video production of the Nassau County Police Department, www.pjads.com/ncpd-hatevideo.htm—Teens talk to other teens about hate crimes and the consequences of committing one. Youth discuss how hateful thoughts can drive young people to commit hate crimes and "cross the line."

Movie

Walkout (2006)—This film depicts the true story of Paula Crisostomo, who along with her high school peers across Los Angeles organized a walkout to protest the education conditions for Mexican Americans in the late 1960s.

NOTES

1. Teresa McCarty, "Language Education Policies in the United States," in *Medium of Instruction Policies: Which Agenda? Whose Agenda?*, ed. James W. Tollefson and Amy Tsui (Mahwah, NJ: Lawrence, 2004), pp. 71–93.

2. Derald Wing Sue, *Overcoming Our Racism: The Journey to Liberation* (San Francisco, CA: Jossey-Bass, 2003), pp. 29–30.

3. Alan Goodman, "Three Questions about Race," *Human Biological Variation and Racism Anthropology News* 46, no. 6 (September 2005), pp. 18–19, www.aaanet.org/press/an/0905/Goodman.htm (accessed May 12, 2010).

4. Quoted in Stacey J. Lee, "Behind the Model-Minority Stereotype: Voices of High- and Low-Achieving Asian American Students," *Anthropology & Education Quarterly* 25, no. 4 (December 1994), pp. 413–429.

5. Vivian Louie, *Compelled to Excel: Immigration, Education and Opportunity among Chinese Americans* (Palo Alto, CA: Stanford University Press, 2004), p. 105.

6. Benji Chang and Wayne Au, "You're Asian, How Could You Fail Math?" *Rethinking Schools* 22, no. 2 (Winter 2007/2008),

www.rethinkingschools.org/archive/22_02/math222.shtml (accessed April 3, 2010).

7. As mentioned in chapter 7, some individual states have passed legislation to make English the official language within their state boundaries.

8. Alejandro Quiroz, "Making Dreams Reality for Undocumented Latino Students," in *The Latinization of U.S. Schools: Teaching and Learning in Shifting Cultural Contexts*, ed. Jason Irizarry with Project FUERTE, in press.

9. Corey Heller, "The Politics of Bilingualism," Bilingual/Bicultural Family Network, 2006, www.biculturalfamily.org/apr06/politicsbilingualism.html (accessed December 26, 2008).

10. Ameena Ghaffar-Kucher, "Citizenship and Belonging in the Age of Insecurity: Pakistani Immigrant Youth in New York City," in *Critical Approaches to Comparative Education: Vertical Case Studies from Africa, Europe, the Middle East and the Americas*, ed. Fran Vavrus and Lesley Bartlett (New York: Palgrave Macmillan, 2009), p. 165.

11. Michael Powell, "An Exodus Grows in Brooklyn: 9/11 Still Rippling through Pakistani Neighborhood," *Washington Post*, May 29, 2003, p. A01.

12. Ghaffar-Kucher, "Citizenship and Belonging in the Age of Insecurity," p. 170.

13. Ghaffar-Kucher, "Citizenship and Belonging in the Age of Insecurity," pp. 172–173.

14. Real Sikhism, "Mistaken Turban: Do Not Relate Turban with Terrorism," www.realsikhism.com/index.php?subaction=showfull&id=1193696645&ucat=5 (accessed February 19, 2010).

15. Real Sikhism, "Mistaken Turban."

16. Quiroz, "Making Dreams Reality for Undocumented Latino Students."

17. Joyce Bryant, "Immigration in the United States," in *Immigration and American Life*, Yale-New Haven Teachers Institute 3 (1999), www.yale.edu/ynhti/curriculum/units/1999/3/99.03.01.x.html (accessed April 14, 2010).

18. Leadership Conference on Civil Rights Education Fund, "The State of Hate: Escalating Hate Violence Against Immigrants," 2009, www.civilrights.org/publications/hatecrimes/escalating-violence.html (accessed February 4, 2010).

19. Ruben Navarrette Jr., "Commentary: No Time for Hate," CNN Politics.com, November 14, 2008, www.cnn.com/2008/ POLITICS/11/13/navarrette.killing/index.html (accessed March 8, 2010).

20. Leadership Conference on Civil Rights Education Fund, "The State of Hate."

21. Anne Barnard, "Latinos Recall Pattern Attacks before Killing," *New York Times*, January 8, 2009, www.nytimes.com/2009/01/09/ nyregion/09patchogue.html (accessed November 4, 2009).

Immigration Debates

At the heart of the immigration debate is the way geographic borders, labels related to immigration status, and human rights intersect to either allow or deny people freedoms and opportunities in a given location. The specific area of dispute is around rights: those that all humans deserve versus those that should be reserved just for citizens or permanent residents of a nation. Human rights are defined by the United Nations as "rights inherent to all human beings, whatever our nationality, place of residence, sex, national or ethnic origin, color, religion, language, or any other status. We are all equally entitled to our human rights without discrimination. These rights are all interrelated, interdependent and indivisible."[1] Although human rights should be provided to people all over the world, there are many nations that violate these rights for citizens and immigrants alike. In the United States the protection of human rights is enforced through the U.S. Constitution, which refers to the rights of its "people," without reference to one's citizenship status. Therefore it is a document that applies to all individuals living in the nation. On the other hand, the rights of citizens are those given to them by their nation's government due to their status. For example, in the United States only citizens and lawful permanent residents (LPRs) are provided with social services such as Medicare or Medicaid and Social Security and are allowed to vote in local, state, and national elections. The immigration debate focuses on the areas where human rights and citizen rights intersect and differ.

THE BORDER DEBATE

"My brother paid the coyote and I crossed the border illegally. It took me a week but it left me unforgettable memories because of everything I went through, hunger the unpredictability of the weather. . . . I was without food and water for thirty-six hours while we waited for the coyote to pick us up at the border. It was horrible!"

—Ricardo, Mexico, 22 years old

"If we put up a wall on the border our country will be a lot safer from terrorists and criminals."

—Danielle, United States, 17 years old

Although the United States has two international borders, it is mainly the 1,900-mile border with Mexico that is discussed and debated, as opposed to the 5,000-mile border the United States shares with Canada. One approach to decreasing undocumented immigration that has received a great deal of attention is the creation of a wall or fence that would span the U.S.-Mexico border. It is estimated a double-layer barrier would cost the United States approximately $2.4 billion in addition to the cost of the labor to build it and the purchase of some of the land, especially in Texas.[2] In urban areas such as San Diego, California, and El Paso, Texas, Operations Gatekeeper and Operation Hold the Line have already erected steel fences with varying impact. One outcome is that border crossers now go through more rural and dangerous terrain and place their lives at greater risk in order to come to the United States. In just one year the United States government reported 473 deaths related to border crossers.[3] The cause of these deaths ranged from exhaustion from the intense heat, exposure to cold, drowning, and car accidents.[4] Another outcome is that undocumented immigrants who make the decision to cross the U.S.-Mexico border seek out smugglers, often referred to as coyotes, to help them successfully cross the border in spite of physical challenges. Coyotes charge large sums of money, often in the range of one thousand to three thousand dollars per person that take migrants years of sacrificing and saving. Therefore, the illegal business of smuggling people has increased at a time when obstacles, such as fences, are being put in place. In order to overcome these barriers, underground tunnels are becoming more widely used to enter the United States. Wildlife may also suffer if such a wall is built, as animals such as jaguars, ocelot leopards, and antelopes will have their natural habitats disrupted.

THE EVOLUTION OF "COYOTES"

Since border crossing has become a business, coyotes have profited from people entering the United States from Mexico. The word has mostly been known to refer to wild animals from the dog family that closely resemble wolves and are common to Central and North America. They roam the desert, but have made their way into urban locations as well. The word started coming up in U.S. newspapers in the 1920s as a term connected to those who become part of the border-crossing process. In 1923 the *Daily News* in Galveston, Texas, wrote, "A new race has sprung up on the Mexican side of the border, referred to often as the 'wolves of the border.'" Similarly, in 1924 the *LA Times* wrote about "a band of criminals on this border, known as 'coyotes,' who live by preying upon persons wishing to secure an easy entrance to the United States."[5] The word *coyote* is the same in English and Spanish and has started to become known for its multiple meanings, in the United States, Mexico, and other Latin American nations.

In 2005 former Arizona governor Janet Napolitano said, "You show me a 50 foot wall and I'll show you a 51 foot ladder at the border."[6] What this basically means is even if the United States does decide to create a wall, people will find ways to get over or around it one way or another. Perhaps the more important issue is not how to stop people from crossing, but how to end the root causes of undocumented immigration, namely, war, poverty, and oppression.

THE EDUCATION DEBATE

"When I get my citizenship, that's my American dream. As a student I need financial aid but I do cannot get it because of that. I also can apply for health care. So, the American Dream for me then would be able to be a citizen, get all the benefits I can."

—Jewel, South Africa, 22 years old

153

HOW WOULD YOU FEEL?

Imagine that you live in a house with a yard and have neighbors on both sides. You each have your own yards and there may not even be any visible division. You likely just know where your property ends and theirs begins. It may also be the case that you have a wire fence that allows you to see each other or a slightly higher wooden fence. However, how would you feel if you woke up one morning to find that your neighbor, with whom you maintain friendly relations, had built a fifteen-foot cement fence to separate your property line from theirs? Would this change your relationship? Could you still ask them for help when needed or just say hello? We can apply this very situation to the U.S.-Mexico border and the message a wall or fence would send, as well as the ways it would change the relationship of the two neighboring nations.

"I want to study to become a chef, but it is very expensive. I have been working to save up enough money but it is really difficult. . . . I just want to better myself."

—Ricardo, Mexico, 22 years old

The United States prides itself on the fact that public education from kindergarten through the twelfth grade is provided and required for all children. However, the issue of whether undocumented immigrants should be able to receive this same educational right has been debated at both the K–12 and college levels. Individual states such as Texas and California have passed or attempted to pass laws that would take away the rights of undocumented children to have a free K–12 public education. However, a Supreme Court decision in the 1982 *Plyer v. Doe* case ruled that all immigrant children, regardless of their status, must have the right to an education through the twelfth grade. Therefore, public schools must accept undocumented students and cannot question their immigration status.

The case for college education is more complicated. Many financial and social challenges stand in the way of undocumented students. Public universities are generally an option for undocumented students only if they offer in-state tuition for students with this status, whereas private colleges create their own policies about whether they will admit students without authorization. And for those institutions who do allow undocumented students to enter, they must show proof that they can pay the full tuition and/or that their immigration status is on file to possibly be changed so they will no longer be out of status.

Unlike the availability of free elementary and secondary education, colleges in the United States are considered a privilege (as opposed to a right) and therefore students must pay tuition. Public universities generally have two levels of tuition, based on where one lives or one's residency. In-state tuition is the lowest rate and is generally provided for those who can prove they have lived or graduated from high school in the state. Out-of-state tuition is for those who live in a different state and is often two to four times the rate of in-state tuition. For example, during the 2010–2011 academic year it cost a Michigan state resident $11,722 for one semester (fifteen credits) of full-time coursework and fees at Michigan State University. An out-of-state or international student had to pay over $29,000 for the same course load.[7] The rates for which undocumented students qualify for vary from state to state. There are currently ten states (although this is subject to change) where out-of-status students living in the state can pay in-state tuition. These states include California, Illinois, Kansas, Nebraska, New Mexico, New York, Oklahoma, Texas, Utah, and Washington.

Since college is very expensive for most families and the rates only continue to rise, students who are citizens have various options for payment, including government loans, also known as financial aid, and various athletic, academic, and need-based scholarships for qualifying students. Undocumented students are often excluded from such options when the funding comes from the government and must therefore pay the entire tuition out of their pockets. This expense, too much for most citizens, is likely what keeps many undocumented students out of college. In 2006 only 5–10 percent of undocumented students who graduated high school went on to college. This is compared to 75 percent of their peers.[8] Only in Texas and New Mexico are undocumented students permitted to receive government funding. In the other eight states in which they are charged in-state tuition, undocumented students are required to pay the fee in full, and in the remaining forty states, they must pay a hefty out-of-state price. When taking into consideration the low-paying jobs undocumented workers often hold, the odds of paying full tuition out of their pockets puts college out of reach for most.

THE DEPORTATION VERSUS REGULARIZATION DEBATE

"I do not believe that any immigrant deserves to be handcuffed and taken to jail like a criminal who did something really bad. If anyone does something wrong they deserve to be punished. But if it is a person who is working and has not done anything wrong, they should let hardworking people make their dreams come true, to help their families, and to help themselves. We are also power for the United States, we the immigrant people."

—José, Honduras, 22 years old

"If people migrate over here illegally, it is because they can't handle the way of life, so to send them back to their country is like sending them back to die."

—John, United States, 17 years old

"They went against the rule and did not earn citizenship like others. I think they should all be sent back home."

One of the largest and most controversial debates regarding immigration centers on what should be done with the millions of undocumented individuals living in the United States. There are various avenues that can be taken. At one end of a continuum of possibilities is deportation; at the other end is regularization, which is the process by which undocumented immigrants can change their status to an LPR. Somewhere in the middle of these two options lies what the United States has done for the past two decades: nearly nothing. Very few changes have been made to national immigration policy and therefore only small-scale efforts have been made to send back, change the status, or create temporary means of living and working in the United States for unauthorized immigrants.

There are individuals and groups that would like all the 11.9 million undocumented immigrants to be deported, or sent back to their home country. They feel such a drastic move would free up jobs for U.S. citizens, cost taxpayers less money in services that go toward undocumented immigrants, and lessen the threat of languages such as Spanish becoming dominant and overtaking English. However, there are certain challenges to such an undertaking. First of all, how would these people be identified and who would be in charge of such a task? Many immigration raids have targeted not only undocumented immigrants, but also people who look like they could fit into this group. Therefore, Latino individuals who are U.S.-born or naturalized citizens have been unfairly attacked in these raids. Furthermore, when police and military place their attention on finding undocumented immigrants, energies are taken away from more serious and violent crimes such as illegal drugs, theft, murder, and terrorism. Second, it is estimated that a wide-scale deportation would cost taxpayers billions of dollars. Third, the number of jobs held by undocumented immigrants is extremely high. The question is whether they could all be replaced. In a 2004 movie called *A Day without a Mexican*, the economy collapsed when all the Latino workers were forced to leave. It is possible that something of this nature could happen across the United States if a full-scale deportation effort would be put in place.

On the other end of the debate are those in favor of changing the status of all undocumented immigrants. In the past this has been enacted with conditions such as length of time in the United States, the payment of fees, and a clean criminal record. Large-scale change where undocumented immigrants can legalize their status is referred to as amnesty. Those in favor of legalizing all (or most) immigrants in the United States feel it would serve to benefit everyone, not just those whose status is regularized. With such a step, companies could no longer take advantage of undocumented workers through low wages and poor working conditions, as they remain silent for fear of being reported or deported. Instead, the salaries of all low-skilled workers would increase, as there would no longer be people who could easily be taken advantage of to compete with those who must earn at least the minimum wage. When individuals get paid higher salaries, they also pay more in taxes. Therefore, the government would see an increase in tax dollars it receives, as everyone would work in the formal economy and earn higher (and fair) wages. Undocumented students who have completed high school but could not afford college on their own would have access to government financial aid in the form of loans and scholarships. Those who have completed college would have the opportunity to put their degrees to use in a variety of fields. As a result, the nation would gain a larger number of educated and skilled bilingual workers, who are central to an economy that is becoming increasingly global and in need of college-educated, high-skilled individuals.

WHAT DOES THE "PERMANENT" IN LPR REALLY MEAN?

Although most people think of undocumented immigrants when discussing deportation, lawful permanent residents (LPRs) with green cards are at risk of being deported too. Until 2010, if an LPR had been charged with a crime, even on a minor scale, they could potentially have been deported to their country of birth. The following are two such stories:

- Sacha Sealey was brought to the United States as a toddler from Canada. He had LPR status and never went through the process of applying for naturalization. He was under the impression that permanent meant permanent. At the age of seventeen he served in the military as part of the Invasion of Grenada and returned home only to suffer from posttraumatic stress disorder, a common condition of veterans. He turned to drugs and had a few minor drug arrests. Following the completion of rehabilitation, Sacha went to renew his green card as usual, but was instead handcuffed and sent off to immigration detention in a jail in New Jersey. After eight months, he was deported to Canada and forbidden from ever entering the United States again.[9]

- Marc was a Haitian-born LPR who had lived in the United States for most of his life. In the United States he was arrested for smoking and possessing a small amount of marijuana. He served his prison sentence, but instead of being released to continue the life he had known, he was sent to immigration jail in Miami. Then what followed was deportation to Haiti, where he was yet again placed in the National Penitentiary in Port-au-Prince, the capital city. Although he was in his country of birth, he barely spoke the language and had only one family member still living there. Despite serving his sentence in the United States, Marc was indefinitely an inmate in a prison where one was lucky to receive food or water and where disease and torture by guards were the norm. When investigative reporter Deepa Fernandes visited the Haitian prison, Marc pleaded with her for his life back. "Yo, I'm begging you sis, just get me outta here. Please. I'm dying in here. They treat us worse than dogs here. . . . I wish I had fought my case harder in the United States, got a good lawyer or something, because now that I am here, they are telling me I can never go back. Ever. All for smoking a joint."[10]

As these examples show, the "permanent" in LPR was really a misleading label that could lead to unknown and unimaginable life changes for immigrants like Sacha and Marc. However, on June 14, 2010, the U.S. Supreme Court made a unanimous ruling stating that "immigrants who are legally in the United States need not be automatically deported for minor drug offenses."[11] As the system currently stands, naturalized citizens are the only immigrant group completely protected from deportation; undocumented, LPR, temporary residents, and visa holders are all at the mercy of the U.S. immigration system when it comes to their fate in the nation.

ANTI-IMMIGRATION ORGANIZATIONS

Groups that oppose undocumented immigrants can be found all over the United States. They range from the American Immigration Control Foundation to the Federation for American Immigration Reform to ProEnglish. Some of these groups have been labeled extremist, nativist, and hate groups by the Southern Poverty Law Center.[12] One aspect they have in common is a patriotic pro-American stance that places immigrants as the enemy. These groups paint an either/or picture that sets up conflict between citizen/immigrant, English/other languages, victim/destroyer, and legitimate/illegal.[13] These types of dueling dichotomies do not allow for areas where the two can come together, as in the case of human beings who happen to be citizens and immigrants or those who speak (or are learning) English plus another language. The "us versus them" context also works to instill a sense of fear of the "other" that creates further divisions.

The Minuteman Project is possibly one of the most well-known anti-undocumented immigrant groups in the nation at present. The organization has the following goals: bring attention and a stop to "illegal immigration" and the country's inability to control the border; decrease border crossing in the areas Minuteman volunteers patrol; and reduce the quota on legal immigration by more than half.[14] The Minuteman Project website is filled with symbols that represent patriotism, such as the United States flag, the bald eagle, stars, soldiers holding rifles with the background of the flag, and Mount Rushmore, the South Dakota mountain with carved faces of former U.S. presidents. All these symbols send the message that being patriotic toward one's nation also means being against immigration generally and undocumented immigration specifically. The Minuteman Project participates in "national awareness to the illegal alien invasion" through speeches, demonstrations, and patrolling the border, often with military camouflage, walkie-talkies, bulletproof vests, and even guns, in order to alert the border patrol about individuals attempting to cross.[15]

THE MINUTEMAN RATIONALE

Jim Gilchrist, the founder of the Minuteman Project, wrote an essay published by the Georgetown School of Law. In it, he listed the following areas (among others) as reasons why the United States needs to step up its enforcement of immigration law:[16]

- Preservation of a long-established American heritage, culture, and language to facilitate commerce and communication, and provide a common bond among the population
- No hospital closures from bankruptcy due to unpaid treatment for illegal aliens
- Substantial reduction in the threat of terrorist attacks against public and private establishments, i.e., schools, temples, churches, businesses, and government buildings
- Elimination of laws requiring the U.S. to support, school, and raise the children of illegal aliens
- Less pollution: cleaner air, streets, and waterways
- Significant drop in crime, especially violent offenses and identity fraud
- Elimination of the thousands of undetected cases of communicable and deadly tuberculosis, leprosy, and hepatitis hosted by illegal aliens who have never been screened before entering the United States
- Better public schools, with smaller budget demands and fewer students per teacher
- Drastic reduction of domestic unemployment rates
- A positive future for American youth

Do you agree that if undocumented immigration were to end or if undocumented immigrants were to be deported to their home countries that the United States would change in the ways listed above?

More than actually having an impact on the number of border crossers, the organization has become the voice of the anti-immigration movement. The media actively seeks them out, and sometimes more members of the media are present at Minutemen border patrolling events than their own volunteers. Thus, the group has created a spectacle around their events and cause.[17]

Jim Gilchrist has claimed that the Minuteman Project is a nonviolent protest, similar to the work of Dr. Martin Luther King.[18] However, as group members have taken issues of immigration into their own hands, they have also been in situations that have placed them on the other side of the law. In 2005 three Minutemen patrolling the border physically restrained a young man they suspected of being undocumented and forced him to hold a T-shirt that said "Bryan Barton caught an illegal alien and all I got was this T-shirt" as they took his picture. Barton was one of the Minutemen who participated in this event. According to the American Civil Liberties Union, "Private citizens cannot detain individuals merely on suspicion that they may have crossed the border without permission from immigration officers. Nor does any law permit private citizens to detain, harass, and humiliate another individual. Allowing such activity to go unpunished sends a message to the entire country that individuals are free to take the law into their own hands."[19] In more violent occurrences, two Minuteman members were arrested and charged with first-degree murder in the case of a father and his nine-year-old daughter not far from the border in southern Arizona.[20] In spite of these incidents the Minuteman Project claims its role in immigration issues is only that of observing, documenting, and reporting infractions of the law.

IMMIGRATION SUPPORT ORGANIZATIONS

The Border Angels was founded by Enrique Morones in 1986 to help save the lives of those crossing the border in extreme weather conditions. Some of the many activities they take part in include setting up water and food stations along the desert areas, advocating for immigration issues through marches and murals, and providing information to immigrants in the United States regarding their rights. Because of the work the Border Angels have done on behalf of Mexican migrants, President Felipe Calderón awarded Enrique Morones one of the country's highest honors: Mexico's National Human Rights Award.[21]

Grupo Beta, founded by the Mexican government, has offices near border areas to support migrants who have been deported after failing in their attempt to cross into the United States. The organization helps three to five hundred people daily and gives them a place to sleep, food, and low-cost transportation to return home. Its mission is to educate "Mexicans about the risks of attempting the border crossing and to provide critical services to the often-penniless deportees."[22]

Mixed Messages

The United States has had a love-hate relationship with the reality and idea of immigration. Marcelo Suárez-Orozco, one of the nation's authorities on immigration, explains, "We love immigrants, mostly when looking back at previous waves of immigration. We are especially fond of glossy recollections of the travels, travails, and triumphs of our ancestors as they braved the improbable journey to this side of the American Dream. In the here and now, though, the feeling is different; immigrants inspire anxiety at best, exclusion and xenophobia at worst."[23]

The drawing in figure 9.1 depicts how the United States claims to put out the welcome mat for immigrants. However, the street sign in this picture, of a family running, sends a very different message. Such yellow signs, often with the word *CAUTION* written across the top, were originally designed by the California Department of Transportation in the 1990s. They were put up to decrease the number of undocumented immigrants who were being hit by passing cars as they attempted to cross busy roads in San Diego as they tried to avoid the border control. The designer of the sign explains, "It doesn't just mean they are running across the freeway. It means they are running from something else as well. I think it's a struggle for a lot of things, for opportunities, for freedom."[24] Although such deadly accidents rarely take place, the sign can be found across the nation as a powerful symbol in the nation's immigration debate. However, the significance of the

Figure 9.1.   Albert Chakhalyan, a sixteen-year-old immigrant from Georgia, illustrates the contradictory and competing messages about immigration in the United States.

sign is also up for debate. Its uses range from being featured on souvenirs such as T-shirts and mugs, to a metaphor for the anti-immigration movement, to a symbol of Latino identity.[25] Regardless of the meaning one assigns to the sign, it undeniably represents the struggles around immigration in the United States.

RELATED RESOURCES

Book

Illegal Immigration, edited by Margaret Haerens (Farmington
Hills, MI: Greenhaven Press, 2007)—This book
provokes debate by offering contrasting points of view
on controversial issues related to immigration. The book
discusses the militarization of the border, the impact of
race on immigration policies, and the connections to
terrorism, among other topics.

Websites

Alienated: Undocumented Immigrant Youth (2005), Listen Up!
listenup.org/screeningroom/index.php?view=6494cc2589
8e091c1d2b212f21af072a#—This short video documents
the daily struggles of a young undocumented immigrant
from St. Vincent who works long hours for meager wages.
The views and actions of anti-immigration groups are also
presented as the nation debates the rights of its out-of-
status immigrants.

Exiled in America (2009), Media That Matters, www
.mediathatmattersfest.org/watch/9/exiled_in_america—
Five siblings, all of whom are U.S. citizens, must make
a life for themselves following the deportation of their
mother to Mexico.

NOTES

1. United Nations Human Rights, "What Are Human Rights?,"
www.ohchr.org/EN/Issues/Pages/WhatareHumanRights.aspx
(accessed February 12, 2010).

2. Blas Nuñez-Neto and Stephen R. Viña, "Border Security:
Barriers along the U.S. International Border," Congressional Research
Service, September 21, 2006, opencrs.com/document/RL33659/2006–
09–21/ (accessed February 3, 2010).

3. MPI Staff, "The US-Mexico Border," *Migration Information
Source*, June 2006, www.migrationinformation.org/feature/display.
cfm?ID=407 (accessed March 2, 2010).

4. James Pinkerton, "In One Year 473 Migrants Perish along Busy Border," *Houston Chronicle*, November 19, 2005, p. A-I.

5. Barry Popik, "Coyotes," *The Big Apple*, October 4, 2007, www.barrypopik.com/index.php/new_york_city/entry/coyotes_wolves_of_the_border_immigration_smugglers/ (accessed February 17, 2010).

6. "Walling Off the Southern Border," *The Week*, November 29, 2007, theweek.com/article/index/29919/walling-off-the-southern-border (accessed May 13, 2010).

7. Michigan State University Office of Admissions, "Estimated Costs for 2010–2011," http://admissions.msu.edu/finances/tuition.asp (accessed October 16, 2010).

8. National Immigration Law Center, "Basic Facts about In-State Tuition for Undocumented Immigrant Students," April 2006, http://www.miracoalition.org/uploads/C0/UP/C0UPMi5ztIxYiBEn6EnoDg/in-state_tuition_basicfacts_041706.pdf (accessed April 3, 2010).

9. Sean Gardiner, "US Deportation Policy," *Newsday* (Long Island, NY), April 4, 2004,www.nj-civilrights.org/literature/VoicesoftheDisappeared.pdf (accessed April 10, 2010).

10. Deepa Fernandes, *Targeted: Homeland Security and the Business of Immigration* (New York: Seven Stories Press, 2007), pp. 27–28.

11. Adam Liptak, "Justices Ease Deportation Rule in Minor Drug Charges," *New York Times*, June 14, 2010, www.nytimes.com/2010/06/15/us/15scotus.html (accessed June 23, 2010).

12. Southern Poverty Law Center, "Blood on the Border," *Intelligence Report*, no. 101 (Spring 2001), www.splcenter.org/get-informed/intelligence-report/browse-all-issues/2001/spring/blood-on-the-border/anti-immigration- (accessed March 4, 2010).

13. Leo R. Chavez, *The Latino Threat: Constructing Immigrants, Citizens, and the Nation* (Stanford, CA: Stanford University Press, 2008), p. 138.

14. Chris Strohm, "Activists Flock to Border, Set Up Citizen Patrols," *Government Executive.com*, March 28, 2005, www.govexec.com/dailyfed/0305/032805c1.htm (accessed December 10, 2009).

15. Jim Gilchrist, "An Essay by Jim Gilchrist," Georgetown University School of Law, 2005, http://minutemanproject.com/newsmanager/templates/light.aspx?articleid=481&zoneid=24 (accessed January 4, 2010).

16. Gilchrist, "An Essay by Jim Gilchrist," pp. 3–4.

17. Chavez, *The Latino Threat*, p. 144.

18. David Kelly, "Border Watchers Capture Their Prey—the Media," *Los Angeles Times*, April 5, 2005, p. A-1.

19. American Civil Liberties Union, "ACLU of Arizona Denounces Unlawful Imprisonment of Immigrant by Minuteman Volunteer," April 7, 2005, www.aclu.org/immigrants-rights/aclu-arizona-denounces-unlawful-imprisonment-immigrant-minuteman-volunteer (accessed January 2, 2010).

20. Bob Christie, "Ariz. Home Invasion Suspects Tied to Border Group," AZCentral.com, June 13, 2009, www.azcentral.com/news/articles/2009/06/13/20090613fatalhomeinvasion.html (accessed January 2, 2010).

21. Border Angels, "Mission," www.borderangels.org/mission.html (accessed April 19, 2010).

22. Fernandes, *Targeted*, p. 37.

23. Quoted in Marcelo Suárez-Orozco's foreword in "Young Lives on Hold: The College Dreams of Undocumented Students," by Roberto Gonzales, College Board, April 2009, professionals.collegeboard.com/profdownload/young-lives-on-hold-college-board.pdf (accessed December 7, 2009).

24. Leslie Berestein, "Highway Safety Sign Becomes Running Story on Immigration," *San Diego Union-Tribune*, April 10, 2005, www.signonsandiego.com/uniontrib/20050410/news_1n10signs.html (accessed May 13, 2010).

25. Berestein, "Highway Safety Sign Becomes Running Story on Immigration."

10 Laws and Policies

The early history of the United States is that of a nation of openness and freedom regarding the movement of people into and out of the country. However, over the past three hundred years the federal government has taken a strong role in the enforcement of immigration issues through the creation of related laws and policies. The approach to immigration in the United States has been "ambivalent and contradictory, and sometimes hostile."[1] National policies and programs have been established mainly to keep certain people out while encouraging others to enter the United States. These policies and laws have continued to change since they were first implemented on a national level in the late 1700s. Many policies use criteria such as race, ethnicity, country of origin, and gender, as well as social and educational factors, to determine who can (legally) enter the nation, become a naturalized citizen, and have voting rights. This chapter contains an overview of key U.S. policies, from the very first regulations in 1790 to those from the 1950s, grouped by category and briefly explained. Although they are each presented in simple, straightforward ways, you should be aware that any immigration policy is highly controversial and complex. Therefore, additional research of any policy outlined here will lead to a great deal of background information, many different perspectives, and much to think about.

"The representative from Harvard said to me, 'It is the ultimate dichotomy. You are illegal, but you want to go to law school.' And I said, 'Yes, that is true. Sometimes you go to law school not to just study law, but to change it.'"

—Jong-Min, South Korea, an undocumented immigrant brought to the United States at the age of one

169

IMMIGRATION POLICIES OF EXCLUSION

Policies of Race

- 1790—The first law about naturalization stated that only "free white persons" of "good moral character" could be naturalized citizens after two years of living in the country.

- 1857—The Dred Scott decision stated that African slaves and their descendants could not become U.S. citizens.

- 1868—The Fourteenth Amendment to the U.S. Constitution stated that anyone born in the United States would automatically become a citizen. Therefore, U.S.-born African Americans would be citizens.

- 1870—The Naturalization Act allowed only White persons and those of African descent to become naturalized citizens.

- 1940—The Nationality Act permitted individuals from the Western Hemisphere to naturalize, thereby favoring White people over people of color.

- 1952—The Immigration and Nationality Act, also known as the McCarran-Walter Act, made it so that race could no longer be considered a factor in issues of immigration or naturalization.

Policies of Ethnicity/Country of Origin

- 1808—Following hundreds of years of "importing" slaves from African nations, Congress ended the practice of bringing in slaves from other countries (although within the United States slaves were still being bought and traded).

- 1882—The Chinese Exclusion Act banned immigrants from China from entering the United States and becoming U.S. citizens. Those in the United States without authorization were deported.

- 1907—The Gentleman's Agreement with Japan unofficially ruled that Japan would disallow the immigration of working-class laborers to the United States and in return the United States would integrate schools with Japanese and White students in San Francisco.

- 1917—The Asiatic Barred Zone Act put an end to all immigration from the Asia-Pacific triangle, which includes nations in eastern Asia and the Pacific islands.

⊚   1917—Puerto Ricans became U.S. citizens.

⊚   1942—The Bracero Program allowed for temporary guest
workers from Mexico.

Policies of Gender

⊚   1855—Immigrant women who married U.S.-born or naturalized
citizens automatically became citizens.

⊚   1907—Women who were U.S. citizens and married
noncitizens automatically lost their citizenship.

⊚   1922—The Women's Citizenship Act made it so that the
citizenship status of women was no longer dependent on their
husbands.

⊚   1945—The War Brides Act allowed for foreign-born women
who married men in the U.S. armed forces to immigrate to the
United States with their children.

Policies of Socialization and Education

⊚   1875—Criminals and prostitutes were banned from entering
the United States.

⊚   1903—Anarchists, or political extremists; epileptics;
polygamists; and beggars were added to the list of people
banned from acceptance in the United States.

⊚   1906—Knowing English was added to the requirements for
becoming a naturalized citizen.

⊚   1907—People with physical or mental disabilities, people
with tuberculosis, "imbeciles," "feeble-minded" persons, and
children unaccompanied by a parent were denied entry to the
United States.

⊚   1917—European immigrants had to pass a literacy exam in
their native language, while Mexican guest workers did not
need to show literacy skills.

⊚   1952—There was a ban on "subversives" such as communists,
anarchists, and homosexuals entering the United States.

The policies listed above give us some idea as to how the
United States viewed certain groups in a positive light and

went out of its way to ban others from becoming a part of the country. Many of these policies have been adjusted, while others have been overturned. Let's look more closely at recent policies that continue to direct the nation's immigration system. Specifically, they include the quotas that determine who and how many people can enter the country, the latest major immigration reform act in 1986 that addressed undocumented immigration, and the policies that followed the 9/11 attacks.

IMMIGRATION QUOTAS

U.S. immigration debates often focus on who is permitted to enter the nation. In an attempt to settle this issue the government has come up with an approach through the implementation of quotas. These rules state the number of people allowed to enter the United States within a specific time frame. Quotas are most often in place for different countries or regions of the world, but they also exist for people with specific skills, those who have experienced suffering in their country, and family members.

The first quota regulations, established in 1921, allowed a total of 350,000 individuals, mostly from northwest Europe, to enter the United States. Other quota regulations were put in place that lowered and raised these numbers and changed regulations regarding the countries of origin of immigrants as well. Latin American nations were not even a part of the first quota system; therefore, people from many countries did not have a way of getting permission to come to the United States until the mid-1960s, when those nations were added to the quota system. And although the Immigration and Nationality Act of 1952 stated that race was not supposed to be a factor in immigration decisions, the reality remained that countries with non-White citizens were disadvantaged when it came to their quotas. The formulas used to determine the number of admitted persons from such countries always resulted in fewer immigrants.

The Immigration Act of 1990 was the last time major changes were made to the quota system. The total for immigrants entering the country each year was raised to approximately 700,000 and was based mostly on the reasons for coming, as opposed to where they were coming from. The visas, or permission, were divided in the following way: 480,000 for immigrants sponsored by a family member who is a U.S. citizen or lawful permanent resident (LPR); 140,000 for immigrants U.S. employers seek to hire; and 55,000 for "diversity immigrants," those people who come from countries that have lower numbers of people living in the United States.

UNDOCUMENTED IMMIGRATION CHANGES

The Immigration Reform and Control Act (IRCA) of 1986 brought forth wide-scale changes with dueling goals: to regularize the status of most of the undocumented immigrants already in the United States and to make it difficult for others to come into the country and find jobs. On the one hand, IRCA allowed out-of-status immigrants who had been living in the country for five years (since 1982) to apply for citizenship, as long as they were found to be in "good moral standing," meaning they had not committed any criminal offenses. This act led the way for 1.5 million immigrants to become LPRs and live more openly and easily as a part of American society. On the other hand, the act also imposed stricter control over borders through increased funding to add more patrols with the objective of making it more difficult for people to cross into the United States without authorization. Furthermore, employers who knowingly hired anyone undocumented would be punished with fines and jail time. While employers were required to check the documents of their workers, they did not have to ensure the paperwork was valid. This loophole created a large market for false and/or stolen documents, especially Social Security cards. IRCA was a policy that helped undocumented immigrants already living in the United States; at the same time it put measures in place to stop more people from coming into the country. However, it does not appear that IRCA was able to decrease the level of undocumented immigration to the United States.

HOW IRCA CHANGED MY LIFE: ARACELY'S STORY

My family came to the United States in 1981 from Guatemala City. We were part of a group led by a coyote that crossed the border in Brownsville, Texas. There we were caught by Border Patrol. They asked us where we were from and my mom answered Puerto Rico [because Puerto Ricans were U.S. citizens]. That's when I jumped in and said, "We're from Guatemala." The agent told her next time to tell me to keep quiet. It seemed like they took pity on us because my mom was pregnant and I was only two years old. The Border Patrol gave our family a car to go back to Guatemala, but instead of heading back my dad made a U-turn. We made it to Providence, Rhode Island, where a large Guatemalan community was being built. That's where we started a new chapter of our lives.

I was placed in a bilingual class and I was taken out for advanced reading. Based on my test scores I attended the best public high school in Providence. I applied to five colleges randomly: Brown, Wesleyan, University of Rhode Island, Harvard, and Rhode Island College. I was accepted to all colleges, except Harvard. I decided to go to Brown because it was a local school, and I would get to stay in Providence and be close to my mom. It was an awesome college experience. What helped me at Brown was my roommate, who had a similar background. I also studied abroad in the Dominican Republic, and there I learned about the Gates Scholarship, which I eventually received. Due to that scholarship I was able to attend Teachers College, where I am completing a doctorate program in international educational development.

I think a lot about how my life would be different if it hadn't been for IRCA passing in 1986. The act allowed my family to get amnesty and become U.S. citizens. At that time I didn't realize the advantages I would have as a documented person. I was never conscious about my status, as there was a lot less public discussion around it. Probably everything would have been the same for me until I started to apply for colleges. I don't think I would have been able to go to Brown. Maybe I would have gone to a community college. I also would not have been eligible for the Gates Scholarship that has helped me pay for my master's and doctorate degrees. I think everything in my life would have turned out completely different.

Although immigration reform is usually determined at the federal level, states can also play a role in creating policies that impact immigrants. One such example is Arizona's Senate Bill 1070, the Support Our Law Enforcement and Safe Neighborhoods Act, which passed into law in April 2010. The law allows state officials, such as police officers, to ask any person they reasonably suspect to be in the state without authorization for evidence of immigration documentation. This law differs from any other because it allows police to approach any individual, rather than only those that were being stopped for other reasons, such as committing a crime. Any individual who cannot produce immigration documents can be detained or sent to an immigration detention center. While this law is intended to impact undocumented immigrants, it could be equally harmful to documented immigrants and U.S. citizens, especially those of Latino heritage, as well as foreign travelers. Following the passing of this act, many government officials, including President Barack Obama, and U.S. citizens and immigrants alike began to protest this bill, calling it unconstitutional. Many believe it would make racial profiling, stopping someone only due to their perceived racial or ethnic background, legal and acceptable. They caution that anyone who looks Latino or is heard speaking Spanish may be unfairly targeted by police.

The effect of this law was felt in Mexico, where the country's president said that it promoted abuse, hatred, and discrimination. A travel warning was then issued by the nation alerting all Mexicans that if they go to Arizona they risk being "bothered or questioned without motive at any moment."[2] Whether this law is found to be unconstitutional, the rest of the United States follows in the same direction, or a middle ground is found has yet to be determined.

POST-9/11 REGULATIONS

The hijacking of U.S. commercial airplanes and attacks on the World Trade Center and Pentagon building on September

11, 2001, have forever changed the way in which the nation approaches international relations. The government reacted to these tragic events by putting a range of new antiterrorism regulations in place. In 2003, Immigration and Naturalization Services, the government organization in charge of immigration, was reorganized and the Department of Homeland Security took over its responsibilities in order to strengthen the immigration-terrorism link. Immigration issues were broken down into three divisions. U.S. Citizenship and Immigration Services generally oversee visas, permanent residency, citizenship, and other issues related to permission to enter or stay in the country. ICE—the U.S. Immigration and Customs Enforcement—was created "to protect the security of the American people and homeland by vigilantly enforcing the nation's immigration and customs laws."[3] While ICE works within the nation, the U.S. Customs and Border Patrol is responsible for enforcing land, water, and air borders. This reorganization sends a strong message that through strict regulation of immigration, there will be a decrease in acts of terrorism. The change in agencies also set the tone for immigration to no longer be about servicing and naturalizing, but about protecting national security. As a consequence, a series of acts aimed to halt entry into the United States for some and decrease or take away the rights of others who were already in the country were put in place.

A number of acts targeted specific groups of individuals. The 2001 USA PATRIOT Act, which stands for Uniting and Strengthening America by Providing Appropriate Tools Required to Intercept and Obstruct Terrorism, created a multilayered and controversial immigration, terrorism, and detention approach. The act denied entry of anyone affiliated with organizations or governments that support terrorism, allowed for longer periods of detention in "immigration prisons" for people suspected of terrorism, and created stricter guidelines for international students, among many other new policies. A registration and voluntary interview system established in 2002 was applied to foreign-born Muslims, Arabs, and South Asians. The result was that over eight thousand primarily Muslim and Arab men were interviewed by the FBI, although none were ever convicted of a terrorist crime.[4] Stricter regulations were also set up to review visa applications and requirements, including the use of biometric identifiers, which use physical characteristics such as fingerprints, eye scans, or facial features to help verify a person's identity. In 2005 the REAL ID Act required anyone applying for a driver's license to show proof of U.S. citizenship or LPR status. The Secure Fence Act of 2006 established stricter control of maritime or sea borders and aimed to reinforce the fencing across 850 miles of specific areas of the U.S.-Mexican border. The northern border the United States shares with Canada was only to be studied.

Post-9/11 immigration regulations were set up in the name of patriotism, as a way to protect the nation from terrorists and their attacks. The effectiveness of the regulations in preventing terrorism was studied by New York University's Center on Law and Security. In 2005 it determined that "the legal war on terrorism has yielded few visible results. There have been . . . almost no convictions on charges reflecting dangerous crimes."[5] The racial and religious profiling, or targeting of specific groups, has been critiqued by many human rights organizations as discrimination and crimes against Muslim individuals or those perceived to be Muslim continued to rise (see chapter 7).[6] Immigration policies following 9/11 have created significant challenges to an already difficult system for all those hoping to enter the country, regardless of their race, religion, or country of origin.

THE EXPERIENCE OF MEXICANS

The case of Mexico deserves greater attention, as it has a unique connection to the United States. Our shared border has not always been in the same place, as territories that originally belonged to Mexico became a part of the United States in 1848 as part of the Treaty of Guadalupe Hidalgo. At that time, Mexico gave up two-fifths of its land, including parts of Texas, California, Nevada, and Utah, among others. In addition to our joint battle over land, Mexicans have a long history of coming to the United States. The United States has had a history of creating contradictory policies that purposefully, and sometimes unintentionally, bring Mexicans across the border at the same time the laws push them back. Let's look at three such policies: the Bracero Program, Operation Wetback, and NAFTA.

The Bracero Program was the United States' response to its decreased availability of workers due to people leaving the country to fight in World War II. Named for the Spanish word *brazo*, which translates to "arm," the program basically dehumanized a group of individuals as only one part of their bodies to represent physical labor. The program was put in place in 1942 to allow Mexicans to work in the Southwestern states in agriculture and railroad construction on a temporary basis. They received meager pay, although it was still better than what they could earn in their country, and faced inhumane treatment and conditions.

Ironically, while the Bracero Program was still going strong, the United States implemented Operation Wetback[7] in 1954. The program was put in place to deport, or send back, undocumented Mexicans living in the United States. However, those affected were not only people who fit the intended description, but also Mexicans who were U.S. citizens, LPRs, and others who simply "looked Mexican." It is believed that an estimated 1.3 million Mexicans were either deported or "voluntarily" left the United States for fear of worse outcomes.[8] Although this love-hate relationship between the United States and Mexicans appears to be a big contradiction, Aviva Chomsky points out that "deportations and recruitment served the same purpose: they provided workers, but ensured that the workers remain 'aliens' without rights."[9]

The Bracero Program came to an end twenty-two years later, in 1964, and brought 5 million Mexicans to work in the United States.[10] For the laborers who remained after the program ended, their status changed from temporary resident to "illegal." What also remained was the demand for low-wage workers who could easily be taken advantage of, and those workers happened to be illegal. While this was over forty years ago, this demand is still with us to this day.

Another U.S. policy that forever changed the migration patterns from Mexico to the United States was the North American Free Trade Agreement, referred to as NAFTA. It was enacted by President Bill Clinton in 1994 in order to strengthen economic ties between the United States, Mexico, and Canada. It was touted as a measure to improve Mexico's economy, as it would decrease immigration to the United States. The three nations were essentially allowed to eliminate borders when it came to taxes and trading fees so that products from one country could be freely sold in the other (this was not the case, however, when it came to people). While the idea may have been to improve the economies of all the nationals involved, the situation for poor Mexicans drastically worsened. Once NAFTA was enacted, Mexican farmers had to compete with the U.S. farming industry, one with higher levels of technology and productivity, and where farmers receive government subsidies, or extra money paid to farmers so they do not overproduce a product and bring down its price. Almost immediately products such as corn and beans from the United States took over the Mexican marketplace and created an uneven playing field for Mexican agricultural workers. Farmers in Mexico earned significantly less money while consumers paid more for everyday food staples. Farmers were forced to either sell or give up their plots of land and many headed north of the border searching for work. It is estimated that over 1 million farmers in Mexico suffered from this policy. More than ten years after NAFTA, Mexican farmers earned 70 percent less for corn and consumers paid 50 percent more for tortillas, a mainstay in the Mexican diet.[11] NAFTA also allowed the United States to build *maquiladoras*, or factories, in Mexico and have the U.S. companies be exempt from paying taxes to the nation while having access to low-wage Mexican workers. While half a million low-wage jobs were created by large U.S. multinational corporations such as Nike, Gap, and Walmart, the competition to keep these factories in Mexico (as opposed to heading elsewhere where human labor was even cheaper) lowered salaries of *maquila* workers over time.

NAFTA did nothing to improve the condition of lower-class workers and farmers. It had just the opposite effect for those individuals and the economy of the nation as a whole. Between 1995 and 1996, the year following the implementation of NAFTA policies, border crossers from Mexico to the United States increased dramatically due to the dismal Mexican economy.[12] The World Bank believes that in addition to displacing individuals from their jobs and homes, NAFTA has worked to widen the gap between Mexico's rich and poor to extreme levels.[13]

Taken together, these three policies and programs show the push and pull relationship the United States has with Mexico and its workers. The U.S. government has had one primary concern that it goes out of its way to protect: the U.S. economy. While no nation can be blamed for trying to improve itself, the question is, at what cost to outside nations and their citizens does this growth occur? What have been the gains and losses for the United States as compared to those for Mexico? These are the issues that the country must address as we move toward new immigration reform and policies.

EXPERIENCES OF ASIAN GROUPS

An overview of the history of U.S. immigration policies reveals the prevalence of discriminatory acts toward Asian groups, especially those aimed at the Chinese and Japanese (although all Asian nations have been impacted). The first policy the United States enacted to target a specific group and keep them from entering the country was the 1882 Chinese Exclusion Act. It was put in place to deny entry into the United States for anyone from China for ten years. It also denied U.S. citizenship to anyone of Chinese ancestry and went as far as deporting Chinese individuals living in the country without authorization. The act was expanded to last a total of sixty-one years, ending in 1943. Such strict and unprecedented restrictions were placed on Chinese individuals because of xenophobia and racism, and because they were viewed as a threat when it came to employment opportunities, especially in the era of the gold rush.[14]

At the start of the twentieth century, the Japanese became the second Asian group to be explicitly targeted by U.S. immigration policies. In 1907 the Gentleman's Agreement required the Japanese government to stop issuing passports to its citizens allowing them to enter the United States. In return the United States, and specifically the city of San Francisco, where Japanese immigration was at an all-time high, worked to undo the placement of Japanese students in segregated (or separate) schools. Ten years later the Immigration Act of 1917, also referred to as the Asiatic Barred Zone Act, expanded the ban on immigration to individuals from eastern Asian and Pacific island nations. In 1941 the United States began internment, or imprisonment, of "alien enemies" who were mostly of Japanese heritage. In 1942, following the Japanese bombing of Pearl Harbor, the United States responded by placing 120,000 Japanese Americans living on the West Coast in "relocation camps," which resembled prisons. The majority of those imprisoned through 1945 were actually U.S. citizens.

The 1940s also brought a slow easing of the harsh restrictions on Asians. The end of the Chinese Exclusion Act in 1941 made way for Chinese people to become naturalized citizens. In 1946 Filipinos and (Asian) Indians could also be naturalized, whereas Koreans, Japanese, and Southeast Asians were still not eligible. Over time different Asian groups were allowed entry into the United States through the end of restrictive policies and the acceptance of Southeast Asian nations, including Cambodian, Vietnamese, and Laotian refugees.

The history of U.S.-Asian immigration has been a difficult one. Many policies and practices were put in place to deny entry and opportunities, and to punish innocent Asian immigrants and U.S.-born citizens. It was not until the late 1980s that the U.S. government officially apologized for this period of history and the unfair treatment of Japanese Americans due to xenophobia and racist reactions. However, many other acts of discrimination toward this diverse group have gone by without recognition of the devastation caused to many.

BECOMING A NATURALIZED CITIZEN

The only way for an individual born in another country to become a U.S. citizen is through the naturalization process. The Naturalization Act of 1906 created standards and procedures that would grant individuals citizenship. This process included application forms, fees, and knowledge of U.S. history and the English language.

NATURALIZATION EXAM QUESTIONS—TEST YOURSELF!

Before becoming a naturalized citizen, anyone age eighteen or older must show that they can read, write, and speak English (on a basic level) and prove they have knowledge of American history and government. Minors who are seventeen years old or younger automatically become citizens with one or both parents. Below are sample questions from each section of the 2007 revised civics exam given to applicants for naturalization in the United States. See how you do:

American Government:

1. What is the supreme law of the land?
2. How old do citizens have to be to vote for president?

American History:

3. Who lived in America before the Europeans arrived?
4. What movement tried to end racial discrimination?

Integrated Civics:

5. Name one U.S. territory.
6. What is the name of the national anthem?

Do you think these are important questions for all naturalized citizens to know? How did you do? Here are the answers:
(1) the U.S. Constitution; (2) eighteen years old; (3) the Native Americans; (4) the civil rights movement; (5) Puerto Rico, U.S. Virgin Islands, American Samoa, Northern Mariana Islands, or Guam; (6) "The Star Spangled Banner"

THE PRICE OF IMMIGRATION

In order to receive government permission to immigrate to the United States or remain in the country under a different status, a large amount of paperwork is required. In order to process the different applications, immigrants must pay substantial fees. In 2010 the Obama administration proposed the following fees for prospective and current immigrants for different aspects of the immigration process:[15]

- $985 application fee for a green card leading to LPR status
- $85 fee for fingerprints and other biometric measures to be taken
- $595 application fee for an LPR to become naturalized
- $340 application fee for a fiancée from another country to come to the United States to marry a citizen
- $1,020 application fee for temporary immigrants to become permanent citizens

OATH OF ALLEGIANCE

All future citizens must recite the following oath at a naturalization ceremony:

I hereby declare, on oath, that I absolutely and entirely renounce and abjure all allegiance and fidelity to any foreign prince, potentate, state or sovereignty, of whom or which I have heretofore been a subject or citizen; that I will support and defend the Constitution and laws of the United States of America against all enemies, foreign and domestic; that I will bear true faith and allegiance to the same; that I will bear arms on behalf of the United States when required by the law;[16] that I will perform noncombatant service in the armed forces of the United States when required by the law; that I will perform work of national importance under civilian direction when required by the law; and that I take this obligation freely without any mental reservation or purpose of evasion; so help me God.

The three primary purposes of the oath are for all new citizens to (1) give up loyalty to other countries and pledge it to the United States, (2) show their commitment to follow U.S. laws and protect the nation (if needed), and (3) follow the principles of the oath.

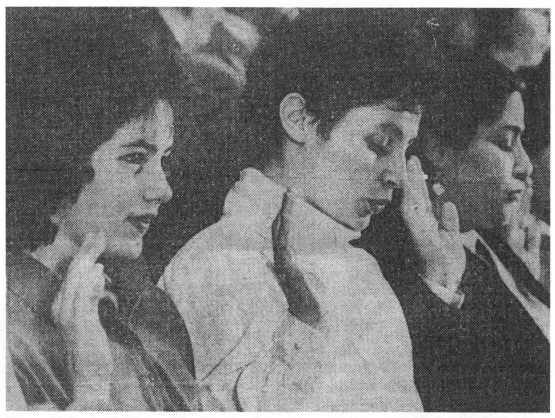

Figure 10.1. A slightly worn-out, yet memorable newspaper clipping of an immigration naturalization ceremony in which my mother and I (at age thirteen) became U.S. citizens. Photo courtesy of *The Pougkeepsie Journal*/Archive Photo.

THE DREAM ACT

The Development, Relief and Education of Alien Minors Act is the full name of the DREAM Act. It is a piece of federal legislation that was proposed in 2001 and has received support (to different degrees) from both the Democratic and Republican parties. Unlike large-scale immigration reform that seeks to find a way to deal with the nation's 12 million undocumented immigrants, the DREAM Act focuses only on a vulnerable subgroup who did not make the choice to come to the United States, but were brought here by families. The focus on youth, who are perceived as innocent victims, as opposed to adults who "broke the law," makes the act less problematic and therefore more likely to see success.

IMMIGRANTS IN GOVERNMENT

Although naturalized citizens have many rights in the United States, there is still at least one position they cannot hold: president. As it stands, only a U.S.-born citizen can become the nation's president. However, naturalized citizens can hold high-ranking positions in government, such as mayor, governor, or senator. The following immigrants have held public office in the United States:

- Lincoln Diaz Ballart (Cuba)—Florida senator
- Jamshid "Jimmy" Delshad (Iran)—mayor of Beverly Hills, California
- Elizabeth Furse (Kenya)—Oregon senator
- Jennifer Mulhern Granholm (Canada)—governor of Michigan
- Mazie Keiko Hirono (Japan)—Hawaii senator
- Vincent Richard Impellitteri (Italy)—mayor of New York City
- Octaviano Ambrosio Larrazolo (Mexico)—governor and senator of New Mexico
- Arnold Alois Schwarzenegger (Austria)—governor of California
- David Wu (China)—Oregon senator

The DREAM Act provides a path toward citizenship for undocumented minors who were brought to the United States at the age of fifteen or younger and have been in the country for a minimum for five years. It states that students who graduate from high school or earn a general equivalency diploma (GED), complete two years of college or military service, and are found to be of good moral character, with no criminal record, will eventually be able to legalize their status. Once the legislation passes, adolescents and young adults who are thirty-five years old or younger (this age limit may change) that fit the above criteria will have six years of conditional LPR status. If they meet all the requirements at the completion of the six years they can apply to become LPRs. Then, following five more years they can also apply for U.S. citizenship.

Many undocumented youth are counting on this bill as their only hope to fully become a part of the United States. If it is enacted it would positively impact approximately 1 million

Figure 10.2. A banner hangs in front of the U.S. Capitol building to urge the passage of the DREAM Act. Photo courtesy of the New York State Youth Leadership Council (NYSYLC).

Figure 10.3. Students head to a rally in support of the DREAM Act. Photo courtesy of the New York State Youth Leadership Council (NYSYLC).

SPEAK UP!

At the time this book went to press in 2010, the DREAM Act had not yet been passed. The following is a letter by Jacki, a college student, who wrote to her senator asking him to support the DREAM Act.

Senator Charles E. Schumer
313 Hart Senate Building
Washington, DC 20510
March 3, 2010

Dear Senator Schumer,

My name is Jacki. I am a resident of the state of New York where I live in a very diverse neighborhood in Queens. I am Mexican by birth and a raised New Yorker. I went to high school in Washington Heights, where I graduated with honors. I graduated with my bachelor's degree in Psychology and Bilingual Education from The City College of New York in Harlem. I am currently attending my alma mater pursuing a master's degree in Education.

My education credentials and dreams should set the path toward a bright future. However, it is a future that comes to a halt due to my immigration status. Being an undocumented immigrant prevents me, and hundreds of other students in my situation, from putting into practice the degrees we have worked so hard for. We are students who have excelled in school and in our communities by being leaders and role models. Yet our dreams of a future in the U.S. have been placed on hold because of the broken immigration system.

Senator Schumer, my dream and those like me are in your hands. You can change my future and the situation of millions of students who are unable to continue their college education or to practice the careers they are passionate about. I ask you to support the DREAM Act, a bill for immigration reform that will allow undocumented students a path for citizenship; and the opportunity to come out of the shadows and give back to the communities that have seen us grow.

I have lived in this country for 10 years. I have my family and friends in New York. I call the US my home. Do not let my dreams be deferred one more year.

Sincerely,
Jacki
A Young Dreamer from New York

How do you feel about the DREAM Act? Speak up and write, call, or e-mail your senators.

young people nationwide. Many undocumented teens lack motivation when it comes to graduating from high school, as they know the future for them is bleak. Students who have the desire to go on to college know that they can only attend certain institutions and that government loans are not available to them. This means they must pay for their education up front and must do so with informal jobs, which usually pay low wages. However, the passage of the DREAM Act could give undocumented students a reason to stay in school and plan for a brighter future. For those students already in college or those who have graduated, it will allow them to put their degrees to use and attain jobs in fields such as education, nursing, and engineering. They will earn more money and also contribute to the society through working in jobs where there are shortages and paying more in taxes as they earn higher salaries. The DREAM Act has the potential to benefit undocumented students, their families, and U.S. society as a whole.

RELATED RESOURCES

Books

Denied, Detained, Deported: Stories from the Dark Side of American Immigration, by Ann Bausum (Washington, DC: National Geographic Children's Books, 2009)—Stories and vivid photographs detail the harrowing experiences of immigrants in the United States who have been mistreated by the U.S. government. The stories of Jews fleeing Nazi Germany, Japanese Americans being placed in detention camps, and the fight for citizenship of Chinese immigrants show the struggles immigrants have faced in the nation.

Brother, I'm Dying, by Edwidge Danticat (New York: Vintage Books, 2007)—The author tells the real-life story of her father and uncle, two men who greatly impacted her life, both as a child in Haiti and then as an adult in the United States. The heartbreaking experiences of both men illustrate how U.S. immigration policies and the country's history with Haiti play out in the author's family.

Websites

Restore Fairness (2009), Restore Fairness, www.restorefairness. org—The short video uncovers the treatment of detainees in immigration detention centers, where there have been cases of deaths and unfounded raids of homes and workplaces. The stories portrayed call for due process and fairness to the U.S. immigration system.

The Least of These (2008), SnagFilms, www.snagfilms.com/ films/title/the_least_of_these/—This video explores the conditions of detainees in the T. Don Hutto family detention center, opened in 2006. This facility houses children and their parents from all over the world who are awaiting asylum hearings or deportation proceedings. The film explores how the United States offers or denies immigrants civil and social rights.

NOTES

1. Walter A. Ewing, "Opportunity and Exclusion: A Brief History of U.S. Immigration Policy," Immigration Policy Center, November 25, 2008, p. 1.

2. Sara Miller Lana, "Mexico Issues Travel Warning over Arizona Immigration Law," *Christian Science Monitor*, April 27, 2010, www.csmonitor.com/World/Americas/2010/0427/Mexico-issues-travel-warning-over-Arizona-immigration-law (accessed April 28, 2010).

3. U.S. Immigration and Custom Enforcement, "About," last revised November 20, 2009, www.ice.gov/about/index.htm (accessed February 4, 2010).

4. Jane Guskin and David L. Wilson, *The Politics of Immigration: Questions and Answers* (New York: Monthly Review Press, 2007), p. 91.

5. The Center on Law and Security at New York University School of Law, "Terrorist Trials: A Report Card," February 2005, www.lawandsecurity.org/publications/terroristtrialreportcard.pdf (accessed March 5, 2010).

6. Human Rights First, "2008 Hate Crime Survey: Muslims," www.humanrightsfirst.org/discrimination/reports. aspx?s=muslims&p=antimuslim (accessed May 16, 2010).

7. *Wetback* is a derogatory term that was initially used to refer to migrants who swam across the Rio Grande, a river that connects the United States and Mexico, in order to enter the United States without authorization. Since then it has been used as an offensive label to refer to undocumented immigrants of diverse Latino backgrounds.

8. Texas State Historical Association, "Handbook of Texas Online," www.tshaonline.org./handbook/online/articles/00/pqo1 .html (accessed January 5, 2010).

9. Aviva Chomsky, *"They Take Our Jobs!" and 20 Other Myths about Immigration* (Boston, MA: Beacon Press, 2007), p. 100.

10. Ong Hing, *Defining America through Immigration Policy* (Philadelphia, PA: Temple University Press, 2004), p. 131.

11. Deborah James, "Food Security, Farming, CAFTA and the WTO," Global Exchange, October 28, 2007, www.globalexchange. org/campaigns/cafta/Agriculture.html (accessed April 3, 2010).

12. Deepa Fernandes, *Targeted: Homeland Security and the Business of Immigration* (New York: Seven Stories Press, 2007), p. 46.

13. Paul Blustein, "World Bank Reconsiders Trade's Benefits to Poor," *Washington Post*, December 17, 2005, www.washingtonpost. com/wp-dyn/content/article/2005/12/16/AR2005121601689.html (accessed February 23, 2010).

14. Michael Brody, "The Chinese Exclusion Act: A Black Legacy," April 17, 2008, sun.menloschool.org/~mbrody/ushistory/ angel/exclusion_act/ (accessed February 17, 2010).

15. Julia Preston, "Fee Increase for Immigration Papers Planned," *New York Times*, June 9, 2010, www.nytimes.com/2010/06/10/us/ politics/10immig.html (accessed June 21, 2010).

16. It is possible to have the part of bearing arms, meaning carrying weapons, or serving in the military for the United States left out based on one's beliefs.

11 Becoming American

"For me American means to be living in that continent. For instance, for people from Europe it doesn't matter if they are in Russia or Italy or France, they are still European. For that same reason, even if I am in Peru or Guatemala or even Canada, I am still American."
—Yadir, Mexico, 24 years old

"Americans are White people, nice people."
—Sabina, India, 16 years old

"I don't know . . . I feel like I hear country music in the background. I want to say that I consider American being something good, someone that believes in freedom and democracy and justice, but at the same time I know that's not true. Not everyone in the U.S. shares these values and it is not what the U.S. necessarily stands for across the world. So I am conflicted what American mean to me."
—Martin, U.S.-Mexican transnational, 22 years old

What does it mean to be "American"? This question has multiple and conflicting answers, depending on whom you ask, as you can see from the quotes here. For many people in the United States, "American" refers to someone from the fifty states. However, as Yadir points out, an American is also someone who comes from North, Central, or South America. Therefore, American is not specific to one nation, but to all the countries that span the American continent. But there are other factors people think about when it comes to being American, beyond geographical location. For some people, features such as racial and ethnic background, as well as languages and accents, also play a role in whether people view themselves or others as American. The feature that is least evident when you just look at someone or hear them speak is their mind-set, or their beliefs and values. In the quote from Martin, he points out that for some people America represents certain ideals, such as those embedded in the U.S. Constitution, but not all Americans may actually share those values. Therefore, geography, physical attributes, languages, and values all contribute to who is and is not considered American, but there are many other factors as well.

Immigrants can decide how to identify themselves, as American or not, but this choice is often complicated by two factors: race and erasing differences. First, if it is the case that "mainstream American" is understood as, or is perceived to refer to, people who are White, U.S.-born, and native English speakers, this leaves out immigrants as well as people of color living in the country. Second, immigrants who select to identify as American may feel that the label forces them to give up their non-U.S. ethnic identity, thereby being forced to choose between two labels, worlds, and identities. For example, Yael was born in Israel and feels that if she starts identifying as American, her Israeli background will become erased. In other words, there is a sense that when one identifies as American, his or her cultural and ethnic heritage beyond the United States becomes subsumed under the larger American label. There are immigrants as well as U.S.-born individuals whose parents or grandparents were immigrants, yet they prefer to take on a hyphenated identity. For example, instead of referring to themselves as Japanese or as American, they call themselves Japanese-Americans or American-Japanese. This allows them to acknowledge their multiple identities. But perhaps this hyphenated identity is needed only because the current perception of what it means to be American is restrictive of differences in racial and ethnic backgrounds. Therefore, we may wish to consider how we can expand the definition of American to include all those who call the United States their home.

Although everyone can choose how to describe themselves, the way in which others perceive them is a different issue that people have much less control over. Sometimes, there is a disconnect between how you identify yourself and how others see you. Below are responses to a question many people are asked on a regular basis: "What are you?" (Interestingly, some people are often asked this question, while others are rarely asked.) The teens' answers and brief rationale for their responses are presented in three categories: immigrant teens, U.S.-born teens of color, and U.S.-born White teens. See if you notice any patterns within and across the three groups.

1. **Immigrant teens:**

◎ *I am Haitian and I am proud of it.* I say this because a lot of people have stereotypes about Haitians, that they are supposed to look a certain way.

◎ *I am an immigrant from a Muslim family.* Everyone knows that I am an immigrant and about my religion from the way I dress.

◎ *I am Black.* I am from African descendants and my background is from Ghana in Africa.

◎ *I am Dominican.* That is my nationality and I am proud of what I am, and not embarrassed for people to know it.

◎ *I am Indian.* I come from India. I am actually Sikh, but when I used to say "I am Sikh" people didn't understand, so I just say overall I am Indian.

2. **U.S.-born teens of color:**

◎ *I am Black.* I consider myself Black because that's my race. I really don't like to be called an African American.

◎ *I am American, but my parents are Ecuadorian.* I answer like this because I look like I am from somewhere else.

◎ *I am Dominican.* The reason why I would answer like this is because I represent my parents and they are Dominicans.

◎ *I am Native American.* I answer in this way because the love I have for my background is amazing.

◎ *I am Hispanic.* I say that because that's what I mostly look like I am.

3. U.S.-born White teens:

- *I am American.* I say this because it doesn't really matter where my ancestors came from. The point is they fought for my freedom and I am now an American.
- *I am Caucasian.* I am White and I am proud, just like African Americans are proud to be Black.
- *I am American.* I was born in America and I am an American citizen.
- *I am Polish, German, Irish, and White.* I say that because of my color and where my family came from.
- *I am American.* I answered this way because I grew up in America and it has made me who I am today.

Although you are only presented here with a limited number of responses from each group, you can probably already see some patterns emerging. The immigrant teens do not self-identify as American, and are often proud of where they come from. The teens also modify their answers based on outsiders' knowledge and perceptions. For example, the Indian student is not understood when he describes himself as Sikh, so he changes his answer because most people are familiar with the Indian label. The teen from Pakistan feels she needs to identify as Muslim because of the headscarf she wears, which marks her as different by outsiders.

For teens of color born in the United States, there is a focus on their racial and ethnic background, as well as their family's country of origin. Only one student quoted here identifies as American, but he feels the need to explain where his family comes from. This may be because, as a person of color, he does not feel he can fully take on the American label, which is often (inaccurately) associated with being White.

For U.S.-born White teens, "What are you?" is most often answered as American. Because these teens fit into the perceived mold of what it means to be American (being born in the United States, White, and English speaking) they have no problem identifying as such. Some U.S.-born White teens do put their race first or their family's ethnic background. One student mentions how he feels proud to be White, similar to how the African American community in the United States has expressed pride in its race. However, a historical perspective shows how White pride differs from other racial groups. The term *Black pride* has been tied to the civil rights movement that began in the 1960s. It was used to bring together a minoritized group in its fight to overcome racism and unequal treatment of those viewed as outside of the mainstream. On the other hand, White pride has been associated with supremacist groups, such as the Ku Klux Klan, who believe in White dominance and superiority over all other races. For the student who said, "I am White and proud," he may not hold the belief that his race is superior to others, like those who have used the term before him. It is possible he is part of a community where White people are the numerical minority and wants to express a connection to the group. But while there is nothing wrong with feeling a sense of pride in one's background, there is a historical difference in how it has been expressed for White people as compared to groups of color in the United States. It is likely that for most White people, they have a greater sense of American pride, as opposed to White pride.

AN AMERICAN ATHLETE?

In the 2008 summer Olympics twenty-three-year-old Lopez Lomong was selected by his teammates to be the flag bearer for the U.S. Olympic team during the opening ceremonies in Beijing, China. At the age of six Lopez was separated from his family as they fled Sudan's civil war. He became a part of the "lost boys" of Sudan, a large group of mostly boys who escaped their war-torn nation after months of walking. Many boys did not survive the journey due to hunger, disease, and attacks by wild animals. Lopez spent ten years in a refugee camp on the border of Sudan and Kenya. He was later resettled in the United States, where he completed high school in upstate New York and went on to attend Northern Arizona University. At the Olympics, Lopez competed in the middle-distance running events for the United States.[1]

While the opening ceremony was a proud moment for Lopez and his teammates, there was talk of whether Lopez was "American enough." Some people thought that because he had not been born or raised in the United States, he did not personify what it meant to be American. However, Lopez had the following to say about being the flag holder and an American citizen, "The American flag means everything in my life—everything that describes me, coming from another country and going through all the stages that I have to become a U.S. citizen. . . . This is another amazing step for me in celebrating being an American."[2] Do you think Lopez Lomong was the right choice to be flag bearer for the U.S. Olympic team?

Looking at these three groups' answers to "What are you?" shows that differences exist across immigrant and U.S.-born teens, just as variations can be found across U.S.-born White teens and teens of color. However, we clearly do not get the full picture of how people truly identify themselves through a question that only allows for a limited answer. Identities, especially for teens, are constantly being developed and changed as they move beyond and between race, ethnicity, and location. Perhaps a better question to fully understand someone is not "What are you?" but "Who are you?"

> "I am an urban, bilingual, heterosexual, Roman Catholic, Puerto Rican male that enjoys listening to salsa as much as hip-hop, who can savor the taste of tostones [fried plantains] as much as a side of collard greens. I can wear baggy jeans, a "hoodie," and "Timbs," put on a three-piece suit with high polished shoes, or a guayabera and Dockers, and fit in anywhere I go. . . . I can talk as much trash about 'yo mamma' as anyone else in my neighborhood, or I can drop some knowledge while spitting/speaking my Spanish/Spanglish slang. My identity cannot be classified or contained into one or two categories. I am much more than just one thing."

> —Joaquin, United States/Puerto Rico, 22 years old, in answer to the question "Who are you?"[3]

PERPETUAL FOREIGNERS

For certain groups, the American identity, or label, is easier to take on than for others. White people are often assumed to be American, though this external perception may change if they have an accent that marks them as foreign born. Many Black people are also perceived to be American, or at least African American, unless they have a foreign accent or dress in clothing such as a dashiki or *bubu*, attire common to parts of West Africa. Of course, these factors (race, accent, style of dress) do not and cannot truly determine whether one is American; they are however, the markers many people use as indicators to make such determinations. Some groups, such as those from Asian and Latino backgrounds, are often viewed as "perpetual

THE "WHERE ARE YOU FROM?" BURDEN

Nabin was born and raised in Sarasota, Florida. Her mother was born in North Korea's capital city, Pyongyang, while her father came from Manchuria, South Korea (currently part of China). Both came to the United States to pursue graduate studies and stayed in the country to work and start a family. While her parents often spoke Korean with one another, they only spoke in English to Nabin, and eventually with each other too. Nabin does not speak Korean and only took it in college for one semester to develop basic Korean. In her lifetime she has visited Korea just once, at the age of sixteen, for a month-long vacation.

In spite of Nabin's American background, whenever she meets new people, and especially when she comes into contact with strangers such as cab drivers or waiters, she will get the question, "Where are you from?" Although Nabin knows the answer they expect to hear, Korea, that is not what she gives them. Initially she will say that she is from Florida, but that is rarely good enough. The response will often be, "No, where are you really from?" To which she reiterates, "I was born and raised in Florida." By keeping her answer within the U.S. context she makes people rethink their assumptions of Asian Americans as immigrants and only immigrants.

Unlike Nabin, Marine was born in France and came to the United States at the age of four. Because of the young age at which she learned English, she speaks the language without a "foreign" accent. As a White person with American English she is rarely asked, "Where are you from?" Sometimes she is asked if people meet her parents and hear their French-accented English. For Marine it is a choice whether she tells people where she is from, as she is perceived to be a U.S.-born American. Although this is a false assumption, it is one people make due to her racial background. However, for Nabin, a U.S.-born citizen, her Asian background places her in the position of constantly explaining who she is and where she comes from, although she resists this questioning through her answers.

foreigners."[4] This view does not apply only to immigrants, but to U.S.-born individuals with Asian and Latino heritage as well. This means that whether they were born in Delhi, India; Springfield, Chicago; or Flagstaff, Arizona, some people may hold the (false) belief that they are both foreign born and not American. This view is apparent when immigrant and U.S.-born Asian and Latinos are asked, "Where are you from?" Sometimes, the questioner is surprised if the answer includes any location that is a part of the United States. This "foreigner perception" is also evident when U.S.-born Asians or Latinos are complimented for their "good English" even though English is their first or only language. Many second-, third-, and fourth-generation Americans from Mexican, Chinese, and Japanese backgrounds, whose features mark them as "outsiders," are often presumed to be non–English speaking foreigners, due to the White-Black racial association many people hold regarding what it means to be (as well as look and sound) American.

There is, however, a very specific population of immigrants in the country who self-identify as American. Their struggle is being recognized by others, and specifically the government. Veronica, for example, has grown up in the United States, but because of her undocumented status, the American label remains outside of her reach. She explains, "I consider myself American. My friends, boyfriend, family, hopes, and dreams are in this country. Thus, I work in every way I can, in every moment I can, to be recognized by the nation I have lived in for so long."[5]

THE AMERICAN DREAM

Being American often goes beyond physical appearances, languages, and values to the availability of opportunities. This is connected to the "American Dream," a term that has been around since the 1930s. It refers to the possibility that all those living in the United States, regardless of their backgrounds, have the chance to succeed economically and socially through hard work. There is the belief that these types of opportunities are not present in many other parts of the world, making the United States a desired destination for many across the globe. It is the reason many people choose to make the life-changing decision to leave their country of origin and come to the United States. They immigrate to the country with the hope that the American Dream will become their reality.

There are many ways to define the American Dream. For many, the dream consists of a well-paying job, a house (sometimes with a white picket fence), a family with two children, and even a pet. But it is largely about living in a country where people are free to live the life they've always hoped for, both for themselves and their children. Most people living in other countries learn about the United States and the American Dream through two main sources: the media, specifically Hollywood movies, and word of mouth from those who are already living in the United States or have traveled there. Table 11.1 gives the expectations three immigrant teens

Table 11.1.   Pre- and Post-Immigration Views of Life in the United States

	Perceptions before coming to the United States	Perceptions after living in the United States
Amadou, Senegal, 18 years old	My expectations . . . well when I watched movies before coming to the U.S., I imagined there would be many tall buildings. When people that traveled to the U.S. showed me their pictures and magazines and I saw the buildings and houses I was like woool!! I knew it was going to be better.	When I first arrived it felt good; I was happy. But at the same time I was having a hard time because I came from a different place so people were making fun of my way of speaking and my clothes. They wanted to fight but I ignored them. . . . I thought about the reason we came here to have a better life—then I met some friends from other places, and some from my own country and they helped me.
Odette, Haiti, 15 years old	My expectations of America came from people that had already been here. They said if you are in America you can get anything you want; it's easy, it's all easier in the U.S. I was expecting that it did not matter who you are and that if you wanted you could have a job, or even a career, money, a house . . . and be free.	These expectations can be reached if you work hard. If you want to be somebody, you fight for it. I think it is so beautiful that we would have many chances to have opportunities and do what we like. I expected to have whatever I want (ha ha ha). Well maybe not, but I will work hard.

(continued)

Table 11.1. *(Continued)*

	Perceptions before coming to the United States	Perceptions after living in the United States
Yamile, Dominican Republic, 17 years old	They told me that here all is good. My friends used to say there was going to be good stuff in the street up for grabs, that everything is for free.	Things were definitely not as I expected! It's not like they tell you how it is. There are people that die to get here—people take boats—they risk their lives and once you're here it's not the greatest thing. They have to think before coming, if you don't have a place to sleep it would be very, very difficult. Once here you have to work; nothing is for free in this country, nothing. If you don't work here you don't go anywhere—for example, my mom, since she got here all she does is work and work for us, because she has her apartment and she needs to pay for everything. Same with us; if we don't challenge ourselves to study to be someone in the future you will go nowhere.

had about the country before they arrived as well as their reactions to the country after having lived in the United States.

Some immigrants feel they are either living or getting closer to reaching the goals they set for themselves upon moving to the United States. However, other immigrants find themselves living anything but a dream, and something that more closely resembles a nightmare. For instance, Veronica was brought to the United States from Mexico as a child with the hopes of living out the American Dream. Yet, she explains, "I believe my mother's experience mirrors the experiences of many immigrants who have come to the United States, led by the fairy tales that exist about the country. Unfortunately, many immigrants have realized that these stories are only fantasies."[6]

"AMERICAN-ISMS"

In the United States there are sayings that reflect mainstream American values and traditions. While they do not represent everyone's beliefs, they have come to be a part of what defines the moral character of the nation, for better or worse. Although referred to here as "American-isms," some of these sayings originated from other parts of the world and have been brought over by immigrants, especially those from Europe, and over time have become a part of U.S. culture. Some of these sayings, and many more just like them, can be traced back to the 1700s, when Benjamin Franklin published them in *Poor Richard's Almanac*. See if you agree with the meanings these sayings hold about the United States and its core values.

- "Pull yourself up by your bootstraps."—This saying refers to somebody who is in a difficult situation and through hard work and perseverance can improve their situation. The focus is on personal effort, without depending on the assistance of others or society. (Values: self-sufficiency, individualism, and hard work)
- "God helps those who help themselves."—This saying takes individualism and work ethic, and adds another layer: religion. It speaks to the necessity of religion, and in this case Christianity, in one's life. (Values: individualism connected with religion/Christianity)
- "Early to bed and early to rise, makes a man healthy, wealthy, and wise."—This saying was brought to the United States by British Puritans. It speaks to the value of hard work and how it leads to wealth. (Values: men as providers, work ethic)
- "A man without a wife is but half a man."—This saying refers to the importance of marriage between a man and a woman and the woman's role in taking care of her husband. (Values: heterosexual marriage, family, women as caretakers)
- "Time is money."—This saying refers to how earning money should factor into how we decide to spend our time. Therefore, we shouldn't waste time, as we would lose the chance to make a profit. (Value: capitalism—an economic system based on privately run businesses and individual or corporate earnings)

DECIDING TO ASSIMILATE OR ACCULTURATE

When an individual, family, or group immigrates to a new country, they are faced with a wide range of decisions regarding taking on aspects of the new country and culture, continuing with or leaving behind their first culture, or combining the two. In the United States the term *assimilation* has come to be known as the process immigrants go through when they take on mainstream American traits as they simultaneously let go of their native culture to appear more American. This relates to ways of dressing, eating, and speaking, as well as U.S.-based values and belief systems that are associated with individualism, competition, and materialism. Therefore, somebody who assimilates to U.S. life may start dressing in typical U.S. attire (jeans, sneakers, suits), favor foods such as sandwiches and pizza, and speak only in English as they reject the ways of dress, typical foods, and language(s) of their home country and culture. They might also look down upon collectivism, cooperation, and simplicity (which differs from materialism). This is all done with the goal of fitting in and being more accepted. Assimilation is a process that can be subtractive, meaning that all one brings from his or her background is taken away and replaced with anything considered American.

While many immigrants either chose to, or are forced to, assimilate, others are able to move between the two cultures that have become their new reality. The process of acculturation is one where people learn to incorporate aspects of their new culture while still including their native culture. This means they dress in ways that fit with mainstream American culture and their home culture, speak English and their native language, eat a variety of foods, and stay true to the combination of value systems that allows them to be who they are. Immigrants' decisions regarding which culture to draw from may depend on what they are doing, where they are, and who they are with. Therefore, while assimilation is subtractive, acculturation is additive in that one culture does not replace the other, but adds to it.

WOULD YOU ASSIMILATE OR ACCULTURATE?

Living in a new country requires immigrants to make many personal and life-changing decisions. Everyone has to decide if they will continue to identify with the culture of the country they came from, if they will drop all that they've known to fit into the "American" mainstream mold, or if they will acculturate to a new reality in a way that brings together the best of both worlds. Read the stories of two teenagers below and consider the ways they acculturated and/or assimilated to life in the United States. Think about which factors played a role in their decisions.

Jesús came to the United States at the age of thirteen with his mother and two sisters from Quito, Ecuador. Although he found learning to read and write in English difficult, within a year of being in the country he was easily able to communicate in English with his friends. When he went home, his mother and sisters would still speak with Jesús in Spanish, but he would always respond to them in English. However, he did speak Spanish when communicating with his family back in Ecuador. Most of Jesús' friends were White, U.S.-born, English monolinguals and some of them did not pronounce his name accurately or simply made fun of it. In order to fit in Jesús decided that everyone should call him John, although his family refused to take part in his name-change decision. While the majority of the students at Jesús's high school were White, there were a handful of Latino students, some from Ecuador as well as other South and Central American countries. Jesús generally stayed away from them and immersed himself with his new friends. He rarely talked about his background in school, although his friends often turned to him for help with their work for Spanish class. After school Jesús took up football and was planning to try out for the junior varsity team. In Ecuador he was involved in salsa dancing, and even performed at different events. There he also played soccer on a regular basis with his friends. However, in the United States neither of those activities interested him any longer, as he noticed that none of his friends respected or cared about either. Jesús struggled with the pressure to fit in with his friends and to remain true to his interests and background.

Mohina came to the United States as a toddler with her parents from New Delhi, India. Her brother was the first person in the family to be born in America. By the time Mohina got to high school she had long, flowing hair that had never been cut, due to her religion, Sikhism. It was a defining feature of hers, yet in tenth grade Mohina made a decision to cut her hair, which had reached the bottom of her back, all the way up to her chin. Her father, who wore a turban and a beard, had never cut his own hair and was disappointed in Mohina's decision. In spite of cutting her hair, an act that directly contradicted with her religious beliefs, Mohina still attended services at the *Gurdwara*, a Sikh place of worship, most weekends and participated in a traditional dance group there too. The *Gurdwara* was also a place where Mohina could be exposed to Hindi, one of India's official languages, as it did not come easily to her. At the *Gurdwara* Mohina wore more traditional Indian clothes such as a *salwar kameez*, whereas in school she would dress mostly in jeans and other typical forms of American attire. She had two groups of friends; the first was made up of mainly White and African American peers in school. The second group was almost all Indian friends that she'd known since childhood from being a part of the larger Indian community in her town. Since they all went to different schools, they got together for special events, including Indian holidays, birthdays, and even trips the families took together. While her parents encouraged her friendships with her Indian friends, they were weary of interactions with non-Indian boys. This caused some friction as she was rarely allowed to attend parties or stay out with her high school friends. Mohina constantly felt pressure from her parents to follow her Indian roots, often in place of that which was associated with being American.

Figure 11.2. These pictures show the difference between typical American attire and traditional Indian dress, such as the *salwar kameez* worn by the young woman.

HYBRIDITY IN U.S. CULTURE

Although the term *hybrid* may bring to mind automobiles that run on a combination of gas and electricity, hybridity goes beyond technology. The following are examples of how cross-cultural interactions have led to the creation of new phenomena that are becoming part of American culture:

- Reggaeton—This genre of music combines influences of reggae and dancehall from the West Indies; Latin American genres such as merengue, salsa, and *bachata*; as well as hip-hop. This new fusion of music has been made popular by raggaeton artists such as Daddy Yankee and Tego Calderon.
- Tex-Mex—This type of cuisine blends traditional Mexican dishes with U.S.-based ingredients. Tex-Mex began in Texas and the Southwestern border states that have close contact with Mexico, and has since spread through the United States. Typical Tex-Mex dishes include chili con carne, fajitas, and nachos.

Hybridity

When it comes to life in a new land, immigrants do not necessarily need to choose between assimilation or acculturation. There is also the possibility of hybridity, which occurs when aspects of two or more cultures come together to form something new. Hybridity generally does not favor one area over another, but builds on the best parts of each. With the increased movement of people and ideas through immigration, travel, and technology, it has become easier for individuals to learn about other cultures and incorporate them into their own cultures.

RELATED RESOURCES

Books

Everything Asian, by Sung J. Woo (New York: Thomas Dunne Books, 2009)—
   This is a novel about family, community, and the struggle for understanding. It portrays the life of a young Korean immigrant, David Kim, and his acculturation process as he migrates to the United States to be reunited with his father living in New Jersey.

The Namesake, by Jhumpa Lahiri (New York: Houghton Mifflin, 2003)—This novel explores the identity issues of a first-generation man born in India who grows up in the United States feeling ashamed of his Indian background. It is only following the death of his father that he decides to reconnect with his Indian heritage.

Movie

God Grew Tired of Us (2006)—This film explores the journey of three "lost boys" as they leave Sudan for America. The refugees build a new life for themselves in the United States as they remain committed to helping their friends and family back home.

NOTES

1. CNN, "Former 'Lost Boy' to lead U.S. Olympians in Beijing," *CNN*.com, August 8, 2008, www.cnn.com/2008/WORLD/asiapcf/08/07/flag.bearer/index.html (accessed September 12, 2008).

2. "Former 'Lost Boy' to lead U.S. Olympians in Beijing."

3. Sonia Nieto, with John Raible, *Language, Culture and Teaching: Critical Perspectives*, 2nd ed. (New York: Routledge, 2009), p. 211.

4. Derald Wing Sue, Christina M. Capodilupo, Gina C. Torino, Jennifer M. Bucceri, Aisha M. B. Holder, Kevin Nadal, and Marta Esquilin, "Racial Microaggressions in Everyday Life: Implications for Clinical Practice," *American Psychologist* 62, no. 4 (May/June 2007), www.olc.edu/local_links/socialwork/OnlineLibrary/microaggression%20article.pdf (accessed May 8, 2010).

5. Quoted in Veronica Valdez, "Walking across the Stage," in *Underground Undergrads: UCLA Undocumented Immigrant Students Speak Out* (Los Angeles: UCLA Center for Labor Research and Education, 2008), pp. 41–46.

6. Quoted in Valdez, "Walking across the Stage," pp. 41–46.

12 Looking Around and Looking Ahead

While the United States attracts 20 percent, or one out of five, of the world's immigrants, many nations across the globe deal with similar issues when it comes to immigration. This chapter will explore ways in which other countries have taken on immigration issues and policies relating to migrants who cross their borders. Below, five nations from North America, Europe, the Middle East, and Australia are described in relation to their different stances on immigration. These are only a fraction of nations with pull factors that attract people to their land. You may want to delve further into how other nations deal with their immigrant populations.

IMMIGRATION ACROSS THE GLOBE

France

France has received international attention for the way immigrants have been treated and how immigrants have reacted to the nation's policies. Immigrants make up less than 10 percent of the population and come to France from different regions of the world. Most immigrants come from other European nations, North African countries (where many of the immigrants are of the Islamic faith), and Asian states.

Many of the immigration issues in France center on the country's struggle to keep its national identity intact. With the increase of Muslim immigrants, a law was passed that targets documented, undocumented, and French citizens alike. The 2004 measure made it illegal for anyone to wear "conspicuous religious symbols" in public schools. Originally this was primarily aimed at Muslim girls who wore hijabs, or headscarves, but also impacted Sikh boys who wore turbans to cover their hair.[1] This law sends a message to those who come from different religious and cultural backgrounds that differences are not necessarily accepted or even tolerated in France. The dissent around such policies could be seen in immigrant protests and riots that have become increasingly more common in the nation. This led France's president, Nicolas Sarkozy, to comment, "France, either you love it, or you leave it. . . . Nobody is forced to live in France. And when you love France, you have to respect her."[2] Instead of acknowledging that change is a part of any country's growing process, the French are concerned with keeping the nation looking and sounding the same. The presence of non-White and non-French-speaking immigrants threatens the racial and ethnic status quo in France.

Unlike the United States, where anyone born in the country is automatically a citizen, France has a different policy. Since the passage of a decree in 2005, anyone born in France to undocumented parents is not permitted to become a French citizen. Therefore, it is their parents' immigration status, as opposed to their place of birth, which determines whether these children are granted French citizenship. This has created a stressful situation for undocumented parents and their children alike, as raids and arrests have become commonplace in schools, parks, and even homes. But more than anything, the decree has created a climate where undocumented parents and their French-born children live in a constant state of fear.

The country also has a law that dates back seventy years that makes it illegal to help an undocumented individual enter the country, remain there, or avoid authorities. Penalties for engaging in these activities include fines and up to five years in prison.[3] In 2008, over 3,000 French citizens were accused of breaking this law, and 363 of those had cases filed against them in this "crime of solidarity."[4] Some of the acts people were accused of, but not necessarily convicted of, included helping undocumented immigrants charge their cell phones, driving them to a supermarket, and assisting them with completing paperwork. France is going after its undocumented immigrants through policies that impact them directly as well as any French citizens who become involved with them in big or small ways.

Spain

Although the history of Spain has not historically been dominated by immigration, there has been a recent burst in the rate of immigration over the past decade. In 2000 only about 2 percent of the nation was comprised of foreign-born individuals, while in 2010 this percentage jumped to approximately 12 percent. These immigrants have primarily come from other European, South American, and West African nations. The fairly recent increase in immigration has been connected to a variety of factors: (1) the low national birth rate, compared to the higher death rate; (2) an increase in the number of available jobs; and (3) a history of relatively tolerant and even welcoming policies toward immigrants.

Spain's approach to migrants has differed from many other receiving nations. For example, all immigrants in the nation, regardless of documentation status, have been provided with free health insurance. Furthermore, there have been a total of six legalization programs that have been enacted in the country since 1985. As a result, over six hundred thousand undocumented immigrants living and working in the nation were allowed to regularize their status. Immigrants from Ecuador, Romania, and Morocco have been among the largest groups to benefit from the 2005 regularization program.[5] These acts of amnesty occurred in the nation with minimal debate.[6] Lawmakers created immigrant-friendly policies because they believed that integration of immigrants into society would contribute to the overall economy of the nation. This was the case for many years, as Spain saw its economic standing rise as more immigrants entered the nation and became documented residents.

However, the positive feelings and policies toward all immigrants have not lasted, as an economic recession has changed the national tone on the topic. In 2007 the Spanish government began running television ads, at a cost of over one million dollars, to deter Senegalese people from making the journey into Spain. The commercials speak of the potential dangers of traveling by boat to the Canary Islands and the deaths and drownings that have occurred as a result of this voyage. The ad states, "Thousands of destroyed families. Don't risk your life for nothing. You are the future of Africa." It also shows a mother, who has not heard from her son in months, speak about his decision to leave Senegal. Then a picture of a man, presumably dead, is shown lying face down in the rocks near the shore.[7] This ad is just one example of how nations who have been open to immigration can change their views and eventually policies too.

Figure 12.1.   A typical street scene showing the diversity in Barcelona, Spain. Photo courtesy of Kimberley Donoghue.

Canada

Although just north of the United States, Canada has a significantly more generous view when it comes to immigration. Nearly 20 percent of the nation's population is made up of immigrants. In 2008 individuals migrated to Canada from Asia and the Pacific (52.8 percent), Africa and the Middle East (14.2 percent), and Europe (14.1 percent).[8] Canada has four major categories for permanent residents to apply for: economic migrants, family class, refugees, and "other" immigrants who do not fit into the main categories. Economic migrants, the majority of permanent resident immigrants, are people who are allowed into the country due to their high levels of education and/or skills, which permit them to work in high-need areas or start businesses. This group has primarily come from China, India, and Pakistan. Family class immigrants are those who are sponsored by a citizen or permanent resident of Canada who is at least eighteen years old. People who are in opposite and same-sex marriages, as well as relationships, are allowed to bring their partner into the nation, as long as they have been married or in a relationship for a year. This differs from many countries, including the United States, where someone in a same-sex couple is not permitted to sponsor his or her partner who is a citizen of a different country. Similar to many resettlement countries, Canada's policy on refugees follows the guidelines of the 1951 Geneva Convention.

Australia

Australia has had a limiting and restrictive history with immigration. The Immigration Restriction Act of 1901 essentially restricted the immigration of non-White people to Australia from the time it was created until 1975, when the act was banned. This led to a more diverse immigrant population entering the nation. In 2006 one-fourth, or 25 percent, of its residents were born outside of the nation's borders. These immigrants mainly came from sub-Saharan Africa, southern and central Asia, and northwestern and southern Europe.[9]

The nation's more recent policy, the Immigration Reform Act of 1992, is one of the toughest in the world when it comes to undocumented individuals. It mandates that anyone who is not a citizen and does not have a valid visa must be detained. This means that many refugees, asylum seekers, and undocumented people, including children, are held in immigration detention centers while their cases are heard. This act has been criticized by human rights organizations, and although it has been slightly modified, the act remains in place.

Australia's detention centers are created for both children and families. In any given year there may be anywhere from 400 to nearly 1,700 children being held in immigration detention centers in the nation.[10] The majority of these children, from infants to seventeen years old, arrived in the country in unauthorized boats, while some came by air without visas. Most stay at these detention centers for over one year, but there have been cases where children had been held for over three years. For children from Afghanistan, 96 percent were given refugee status due to the persecution they faced from the Taliban and were freed from detention between the years of 1999–2003.

Indians from South Asia make up a significant percentage of the foreign-born international student population in Australia, second only to students from China. These students bring a great deal of money into the country through the higher international student tuition rates they pay. In 2009 a pattern began to develop, with Indian students in the city of Melbourne being violently attacked with knives and screwdrivers. These acts, referred to by some as "curry bashing" or "Indian hunting," have been called anti-Indian and racist by many groups.[11] Yet the city is working to discredit such claims and has put a great deal of money into ads to entice international students to study in the country, as they are important for the Australian economy. One can draw a connection between these incidents against Indians and Australia's 1901 Immigration Restriction Act, where there was a push to keep out non-Whites. The nation is still struggling with its increased diversity,

IMMIGRATION DETENTION IN AUSTRALIA

Here you will find the experiences of two teenage boys who made it to Australia only to be placed in detention centers. They were later released because it was determined that they were refugees. They speak of the uncertainty, difficult conditions, and daily life in detention.

"When we arrived the officers took us by bus to Darwin [an immigration detention center] and then the interview started. There was no interpreter for us. People who couldn't speak, they just . .. they asked our names and whoever could answer it, they answered them. And then they said 'you are here illegally so you will be detained' and then after they took us to the camp. . . .When we arrived [at the detention centre] they give us just one piece of sandwich until the next morning. After 6 hours [we got] meat, rice, I think, I forgot. No drink, nothing else, no fruits."

—Teenage unaccompanied boy found to be a refugee[12]

"I can tell you that things are very, very difficult for us. I can say that you can never call that place a detention centre. It was of course a prison. . . . Even in prison you know at least for how long you will be in prison, but in a situation like that we did not know what was happening next. We did not know how long we would be spending in this place. And most of the time our roommates and the people who used to live with us, they were getting changed every three weeks or every two weeks, the people that we were getting around for a while they used to go and then some new people would replace them. And sometimes they would put the new arrivals with the people who have been there for a quite a long time who have completely lost their minds and their ability to think and when you spend some time with people like that who have been out of their minds so of course you lose your mentality, and you lose your thoughts as well and this is what was happening to us. Sometimes I was looking at those people I was thinking that we'll all end up in the same place so in short, I can say life was very horrible."

—Unaccompanied Afghan boy found to be a refugee[13]

and the way Australia handles the treatment of its Indian students will likely set the path for future immigration policies.

United Arab Emirates (UAE)

The percentage of immigrants in the UAE is over 80 percent. This makes the young nation, founded in 1972, a unique case where the overwhelming majority of the country's residents are considered to be "outsiders." However, this statistic is misleading, as the way immigrant is defined in the UAE differs from most nations. In the UAE, being born in the country does not ensure citizenship. Children born in the UAE are only entitled to Emirati citizenship if their father is a citizen. Anyone who is not a citizen is a temporary resident of the country. Citizens, a minority of the population, are provided with free access to health care and education through the college level. As a result, immigrants must pay for all their medical expenses and schooling.

Because the UAE is a young and growing country, many immigrants from Southeast Asia and India have been brought in to provide cheap labor. The workforce has been especially focused on construction, where workers have endured awful conditions such as below-minimum-wage pay, work weeks that may require eighty hours of labor, and housing that may require men to live in large groups in huts without running water or electricity. These conditions are especially harsh when considering the economic situation of the UAE, which, as a wealthy nation, can more than afford to provide humane conditions for its workers. Furthermore, immigrant workers are denied the right to join or form a union, which can fight for workers' rights. The UAE leaves many immigrants who came to the nation to work with little to no means to stand up for themselves and earn fair wages that would allow them to live in decent conditions.

The people in the UAE who are considered immigrants are those born in other countries, such as India, Pakistan, China, and the Philippines, as well as those born in the UAE whose ethnic background is not Emirati. These strict citizenship guidelines have created a situation where second- and third-generation UAE-born individuals are still considered immigrants in the only country they've ever known to be their home. This poses a challenge because in certain cases after a family has been out of their country of heritage for a few generations they may no longer be recognized as citizens there any longer. Therefore, if the immigration laws are not changed in the nation, future generations will continue to live as second-class residents and may even be stateless people who are not recognized as citizens in any nation.

MOVING FORWARD

The United States has many decisions to make in terms of how it will move ahead with immigration. The public is united in its belief that the country needs to reform the immigration system. A poll found that 8 percent feel that minor changes are needed, 45 percent believe that significant changes need to be made, and 44 percent think the immigration system needs to be completely reconstructed.[14] However, that is where the agreements end. The main area of difference and disagreement among the U.S. population stems from what those changes in immigration laws and policies should include. In order to begin the reform process, we can look at what has occurred over the nation's history, look at what other countries have done, and/or try approaches that are completely new and innovative. The question about the direction we should take as a nation is a complex one with multiple and varied viewpoints. Below are the views of a range of teens on subtopics that are a part of the nation's larger immigration debate. See if you agree or disagree with their views, or have different perspectives on the solutions to these issues.

Undocumented Immigration

"If you're gonna give every immigrant the legalization you're gonna make America the land of crashers or disaster, not the land of opportunities."
—Andrei, Georgia, 16 years old

215

"It's not good. The papers are necessary in America. If people don't have papers they should go to jail because it's not good; it's illegal."

—Badrya, Pakistan, 18 years old

"Probably if there was a way to increase the number of jobs that would be great. Unfortunately, there is a crisis and it's hard to accomplish this. I think those immigrants [without documentation] who are already here, if they cannot find a job in this country like for a certain amount of time, they probably should try to find a job in their country."

—Stas, Uzbekistan, 16 years old

"Those people that don't have their papers obviously come because they want a better life. Some people say you should put them back, but I don't think so. If their country was in good condition they wouldn't have to come to America to try a new life. I would say don't ship them back to their country because they come for a good reason, to have a better life. If your country is good, why leave for something else?"

—Flore, Haiti, 16 years old

"I would recommend that everyone in the country that is undocumented have a pathway to legalization because everyone deserves that chance. I know that the fact that my parents got that chance made me have a more stable life."

—Martin, U.S.-Mexico Transnational, 22 years old

One of the largest questions that the nation must deal with is what to do with the approximately 12 million undocumented immigrants living in the United States. The teen perspectives presented here span the diverse views of ways to deal with undocumented immigrants in the United States. There are people who feel that allowing them to stay in the nation would pose a risk to maintaining the power of the United States. Along the same lines, there are people who simply feel they have committed a crime and should be imprisoned or sent back to their home country. Andrei's perspective occupies a middle ground, giving everyone a chance to see if they can find employment, and based on that criteria deciding if they can remain in the country or need to return to their place of birth. The final solution is to allow any undocumented immigrant in the country permission to stay due to the difficult circumstances they likely left behind. Amnesty and regularization pathways, such as those in the history of the United States and Spain, are examples of programs that allow for undocumented immigrants to change their status.

Quota Systems

Another area that is constantly being debated when it comes to immigration is who should be allowed to immigrate to the United States. This includes numbers of people, as well as their country of origin, educational level, and area of employment. Below, a group of high school students discuss the possible factors the nation should consider when handing out green cards and visas:

Student 1: We should select people based on their education, on their background, how they are raised.

Student 2: Not really, because your background don't [*sic*] define who you are.

Student 3: America needs educated people, so they should be educated.

Student 4: But people need help, and many of the people that need help may not be educated.

For the students above, the main struggle over who to allow in the United States is between those people who are highly educated and work in high-skilled and high-need areas versus those who likely have low levels of formal education, come from poverty, and may come from countries where they are oppressed or persecuted in one way or another. Thus, the question is whether to allow mostly skilled and educated immigrants, those who are poor and can work in low-skilled jobs, or a combination of the two groups, as well as others.

Officialization of English

"No, English should not become the official language because everybody has a language and that is good that there are many different languages and they can help others by speaking other languages. And for people who can only speak English, they should learn other languages; that is better."

—Candida, Dominican Republic, 16 years old

"It would help and it would not. It some ways it would help because while making English the official language people will learn English faster and some people that's not interested in learning English will learn because they have to, but in some other ways it would be hard for immigrants that are just coming here to learn the language."

—Flore, Haiti, 16 years old

"This is America and everyone should speak English. It makes sense to have English as the official language."

—Elena, Ukraine, 19 years old

While English is the dominant language of the United States, it is not the official national language. There are people who believe legislation to give English official status in the United States is needed. The debate around the "officialization" of English involves the degree to which immigrants will be allowed or encouraged to become bi- or multilingual and continue to speak their native language. It also brings up the question of whether a nation needs just one language to define itself, or whether multilingualism is equally viable for a nation of immigrants to characterize themselves. While there seems to be a consensus that English matters, the larger question is whether it's English only or English plus that will become the language policy of the United States.

International Policies

"I recommend we look at how trade policies affect other countries and how they cause immigrants to come to the U.S. and not just ignore the fact. This phenomena comes from somewhere; there is a reason why people come here. There is a reason why there is poverty in other countries and we need to recognize that."

—Martin, U.S.-Mexico Transnational, 22 years old

"Tightening borders may slow illegal immigration, but it is not a solution. . . . If we look at the big picture, however, the only long-term solution to illegal immigration is to think globally and realize the problem extends beyond our borders. To do this, we need to help neighboring countries balance their population growth with their resources, including food and housing. In this regard, the United States can play an important leadership role by providing direct help and by being a good role model."

—Kate, United States[16]

Immigration is not a national issue, but a transnational phenomenon. This means that immigration is not just an outcome of what happens in one country, but how countries interact and what happens in between. Any policy made in the United States will have an impact on other places in the world, and these policies often play a role in increasing or decreasing the movement of people across borders. We have already seen how policies like NAFTA (see chapter 10) that are not directly related to immigration can change immigration flows. Thus, policies related directly to immigration, as well as those tied to economics, trade, and security, all impact immigration, whether directly or indirectly, intentionally or unintentionally.

The subtopics of the immigration debate addressed in this chapter are just a few of the many areas that comprehensive immigration reform may attempt to tackle. Other areas may include the U.S.-Mexico border, the DREAM Act, and enforcement, just to name a few. Where do you stand on these issues? The democratic nature of the United States allows for everyone's voice to be heard. Even if you are not yet old enough to vote, or cannot vote due to your citizenship status, you can still share your views on the highly controversial topic of immigration. Below you will find websites for blogs and forums where you can post your views and interact with others. Become an advocate, fight for what you believe in, and pave the way for the United States to continue with its rich immigrant past, present, and future.

RELATED RESOURCES

Blogs and Websites

- America's Voice—americasvoiceonline.org/blog/
- Center for Immigration Studies—www.cis.org/ImmigrationBlog
- Change.org—immigration.change.org/
- Citizen Orange—www.citizenorange.com/orange/
- Damn Mexicans—damnmexicans.blogspot.com/
- Dream Activist—www.dreamactivist.org/
- FAIR (Federation for American Immigration Reform)—www.fairus.org/
- Immigration Impact—immigrationimpact.com/
- Immigration 2050—imagine2050.newcomm.org/
- International Rescue Committee—www.theirc.org/
- La Frontera Times—www.lafronteratimes.com/
- Media Matters for America—mediamatters.org/blog/
- MATT (Mexicans and Americans Thinking Together)—matt.org/english/blog/index.html
- Minuteman Project—www.minutemanproject.com/
- NYSYLC (New York State Youth Leadership Council)—www.nysylc.org/

◎ **Political Teen Tidbits—frecklescassie.wordpress.com/
   category/immigration/**

◎ **Project Economic Refugee—www.economicrefugee.net/**

◎ **Colorlines News for Action—www.colorlines.com/**

◎ **Vivir Latino—vivirlatino.com/**

NOTES

1. Kimberly Hamilton and Patrick Simon, with Clara Veniard, "The Challenge of French Diversity," Migration Information Source, November 2004, www.migrationinformation.org/Profiles/display. cfm?ID=266 (accessed May 2, 2010).

2. Patrice de Beer, "France's Immigration Policies," Open Democracy, February 12, 2007, www.opendemocracy.net/ globalization-institutions_government/france_immigration_4338.jsp (accessed April 28, 2010).

3. Claudia Núñez, "France Deports Children of Undocumented Immigrants," New American Media, December 1, 2009, news.newamericamedia.org/news/view_article.html?article_id=043c7 2df4d3a00d47d365f11524801c9 (accessed December 2, 2009).

4. Caroline Brothers, "French Deputies Decline to Quash Measure on Aiding Migrants," *New York Times*, May 5, 2009 www.nytimes.com/2009/05/06/world/europe/06iht-refuge.html (accessed August 6, 2009).

5. Joaquín Arango and Maia Jachimowicz, "Regularizing Immigrants in Spain: A New Approach," Migration Information Source, September 2005, www.migrationinformation.org/Feature/ display.cfm?ID=331 (accessed May 2, 2010).

6. Jason DeParle, "Spain, Like U.S., Grapples with Immigration," *New York Times*, June 10, 2008, www.nytimes.com/2008/06/10/ world/europe/10migrate.html?pagewanted=1&_r=2&hp (accessed August 6, 2009).

7. "Spain Begins Anti-Migration Ads," *BBC News*, September 20, 2007, news.bbc.co.uk/2/hi/africa/7004139.stm (accessed May 2, 2010).

8. Citizenship and Immigration Canada, "Facts and Figures, Immigration Overview Permanent and Temporary Residents," 2008, www.cic.gc.ca/english/pdf/research-stats/facts2008.pdf (accessed April 21, 2010).

9. "Migration," Australian Bureau of Statistics, 2005–2006, p. 9.

10. Australian Human Rights Commission, "A Last Resort?" National Inquiry into Children in Immigration Debate," May 13, 2004, www.humanrights.gov.au/human_rights/children_detention_report/report/chap03.htm (accessed May 4, 2010).

11. Madelene Pearson and Rebecca Keenan, "Indian Students Targeted in Melbourne Attacks," Bloomberg, June 9, 2009, www.bloomberg.com/apps/news?pid=20601109&sid=aPsONvqy_SAs (accessed May 8, 2010).

12. Australian Human Rights Commission, "A Last Resort?

13. Australian Human Rights Commission, "A Last Resort?"

14. Randal C. Archibold, Megan Thee-Brenan, "Polls Show Most in U.S. Want Overhaul of Immigration Laws," *New York Times*, May 3, 2010, www.nytimes.com/2010/05/04/us/04poll.html (accessed May 8, 2010).

15. Kate, "Ending Illegal Immigration," Teen Ink, December 17, 2009, www.teenink.com/opinion/all/article/49477/Ending-Illegal-Immigration/ (accessed May 8, 2010).

Index

Index

Index

About the Author

Tatyana Kleyn is an immigrant from the Soviet Union
(currently Latvia). She is assistant professor in the Bilingual
Education and Teaching English to Speakers of Other
Languages program at The City College of New York. In 2007
she received an EdD in international educational development
at Teachers College, Columbia University. Tatyana is the
coauthor of *Teaching in Two Languages: A Guide for K–12
Bilingual Educators* with Sharon Adelman Reyes (Corwin
Press, 2010). She has also written about the cultural, linguistic,
and educational needs of the Garífuna people in Honduras.
Tatyana was an elementary school teacher in San Pedro Sula,
Honduras, and Atlanta, Georgia.